Lucie Lamy

egyptian mysteries

New light on ancient knowledge

With 173 illustrations, 14 in colour

Thames and Hudson

To R. A. Schwaller de Lubicz,
my teacher, to whom I owe
everything

ART AND IMAGINATION
General Editor: Jill Purce

Translated from the French by Deborah Lawlor
Picture research by Vanessa Whinney

© 1981 Lucie Lamy
Reprinted 1989

Filmset in Great Britain by Keyspools Ltd,
Golborne, Lancashire
Printed and bound in Japan

Contents

Prologue: the Nile

Hapy – The Nile

They come, the waters of life which are in the sky,
They come, the waters of life which are in the earth ...
The sky is aflame for you, the earth trembles for you, before the
divine birth [of Osiris–Nile]. The two mountains are split apart.
The god comes into being, the god has power in his body ...
The month is born, the fields live. (Pyramid Texts, 2063.)

Egypt is the work of the Nile. First it hollowed out its bed in
the immense plateau of desert limestone and sandstone.
Then, during the course of thousands of years, it deposited
its alluvium at the bottom of the narrow valley, forming
the arable ground. It was on the Nile, and on the amplitude
of its annual flood, that the entire life of ancient Egypt
depended; for rain is very rare. Egypt can look like a lush
oasis if the Nile flood comes 'in its day', or else a country
made desolate by famine if the river fails to rise or if its
rising is insufficient. The Nile's behaviour was carefully
studied and the celestial signs accompanying its annual
flood were minutely observed and recorded.

Egypt is the image of the skies, where the divine beings
sail the 'waters on high'; and so the Nile has a heavenly as
well as an earthly source. Its flood transforms Egypt into a
vast sea, likened to the primordial ocean, the Nun. The Nile
is thus an integral part of myth. Its periodic rise and fall are
associated with the myth of Osiris, divine principle of
perpetual return, death and rebirth, as symbolized by the
annual cycle of vegetation.

Ancient travellers to Egypt were told by the priests that
the source of the Nile was at the first cataract, at Bigah or
Elephantine, where the river surged forth from the Calf (or
Lower Leg) of Osiris, the divine relic preserved here. But as
it is well known that the banks of the Nile *upstream* from
Elephantine are dotted with ancient Egyptian temples, it is
obvious that the source was known to be much further
beyond, to the south.

O Osir! The inundation is coming; abundance rushes in,
The flood-season is coming, arising from the torrent issuing from
Osir. (O King) may Heaven give birth to thee as Orion! (Pyramid
Texts 1944, 2113–2117.)

The Pyramid Texts tell us that Osiris, son of Nut, the Sky,
and Geb, the Earth, inherited his father's throne, but was
overthrown by his brother Seth, principle of discord.
Plutarch transmits the whole legend as follows:

In the very distant past, after having completely organized and
civilized the land of Egypt, Osiris confided the care and governing
of the country to Isis, his sister, and left for the south in order to
teach agriculture, the laws of harmony, and the ways of
worshipping the divine powers, to the still savage peoples of
those regions.

When, after a long absence, Osiris returned to Egypt, Seth and
his seventy-two accomplices trapped him in an ambush. They
enclosed him in a coffin made to fit his dimensions and they
threw it into one of the arms of the Nile. It was carried out to sea
and floated northward until the waves washed it ashore at Byblos
in Lebanon. A magnificent tree grew up around the coffin, and
the king of that country, when he heard of this marvel, had the
tree cut down to make a column in his palace.

Isis, meanwhile, having heard from the whispers of the winds
what had become of Osiris, set out in search for him. Arriving one
day at Byblos, and transformed into a swallow, she flew around
and around the column. Finally she succeeded in bringing the
sarcophagus back to Egypt, where she hid it in a remote part of
the Delta. But one night when Seth was hunting by the full moon
he discovered it, seized the body of Osiris, cut it into fourteen
pieces and scattered them all over the country.

So Isis, aided by her sister Nepthys, set out in quest of the parts
of Osiris' body. As she found each part, she buried it in the place
where it had come to rest, as a sacred relic. Thus, the head was
preserved in a reliquary at Abydos, an ear was to be found at Sais
in the Delta, and the left lower leg, the Calf of Osiris, on the Isle of
Bigah where, as the legend says, the sources of the Nile spring
forth.

A bas-relief in the temple adjoining the Nilometer on
the nearby island of Philae shows the sources of the Nile
symbolically. A serpent's body outlines a cave in some
rocks, within which Hapy, the personification of the Nile,
pours water from the two vases he holds in his hands. One
cannot help but be struck by the coincidence that the
zodiacal sign of Aquarius (the Waterbearer) is symbolized
by the vase, and that the lower leg, which is the part of the
body assigned to its influence in astrology, is enshrined as
the local relic.

According to Plutarch, the Egyptians saw the Nile as an outflow of Osiris and the earth as the body of Isis. Thus, in becoming intermixed with the soil, the Nile-Osiris fecundates the Earth-Isis. The most enlightened among the priests, he says, specify that Osiris is the principle of all that which is humid, the power and cause of all generation, the substance of every seed, the definitive symbol of all death and rebirth. Inversely, Seth-Typhon is the principle of all that which burns, consumes. He has red hair, for example, for he represents the desert rocks, arid and sterile.

The ambush laid by Seth-Typhon for Osiris, continues Plutarch, represents the intensity of dryness which evaporates the Nile's waters and narrows them to the riverbed. The presence among Seth's accomplices of the Ethiopian queen Aso represents the burning south winds which indeed blow during the months preceding the flood. Likewise the stifling of Osiris in his coffin represents the low water-mark which, in Egypt, is exceptionally important. The flood itself symbolizes Osiris's annual resurrection.

constellation of Orion, which appears just before the Dog Star (Sirius), is assigned to Osiris.

Such legends as these, based on actual facts, reflect the unique nature of the Nile: 6700 kilometres (over 4000 miles) long, a sixth of the earth's circumference, and capable at its flood of providing a massive flow of water, sixty times greater than its normal volume, after covering a stretch of more than 1000 kilometres (over 600 miles) without a single tributary. Throughout history it has incited admiration by the breadth and contemplative majesty of its flow, and curiosity by its exceptional rhythm. Contrary to other rivers, it begins its annual swelling in the hottest time of the year, at the beginning of the Dog Days, that is, at the moment when Sirius rises at the same time as the sun, a date which during the third millennium BC coincided with the summer solstice.

This coincidence between the heliacal rising of Sirius and the beginning of the inundation marked, from the earliest moments of Pharaonic history, the beginning of

In the Temple of Philae the inundation is pictured in a bas-relief in which the Nile, described as 'Hapy, Father of the Neterw' (divine entities), again with two streams of water, moistens a basin in which plants are growing. In this basin stands 'the soul of Osiris', the human-headed Benu bird, the phoenix, itself a symbol of the Nile flood and of the incessant cycles of rebirth. Next to this scene 'Horus, Son of Isis' holds a triple palm, sign of the new year which begins with the inundation, and three vases from which flows a stream of *ankh* symbols or 'keys of life', flanked by two streams of water. Horus has assumed for this occasion the ibis head, characteristic of Thoth, Master of Time, whose name belongs to the first month of the year. Horus makes libation 'to his father Sokar-Osiris', who is followed by his two sisters, Isis and Nepthys.

According to a tradition transmitted by the Coptic calendar still in use during the last century, the Nile's flood was announced during the 'Night of the Drop' at which time a 'tear of Isis, coming from Heaven, falls in the river, causing it to swell'. Plutarch writes that the souls of the divine entities shine in the stars: 'Sirius is the one consecrated to Isis, for it brings the water.' Similarly, the

the year, as is witnessed by this small ivory tablet which belonged to the second king of the First Dynasty. On it is inscribed, 'Sirius, Opener of the year, Inundation, 1'. Isis-Sirius is represented by a cow wearing the symbol of the year between its horns; this same symbol is found employed again three thousand years later in the famous circular zodiac at Dendera.

Given the accurate correspondences between the myth and the Nile's actual behaviour, one naturally begins to suspect that the priests really knew more about its sources than their continued insistence on the Bigah story would suggest.

The Egyptians' geographical knowledge seems to have been extensive. Regarding northern regions, the myth has Osiris' coffin arrive at Byblos, exactly the place where Adonis is the subject of a legend analogous to that of Osiris. The Egyptians were already going there by the First Dynasty (c. 3200 BC) to obtain wood for construction. As for the south, the myth takes Osiris to 'still savage' regions. The existence of ivory and ebony among the funerary objects of the first historic kings bears witness at least to commercial exchanges with central Africa at that time.

Furthermore, documents show that a nobleman of the Old Kingdom (after 2800 BC) brought back a 'dancing dwarf' from the south who is thought to have been a Pygmy. Since the Pygmies inhabited regions neighbouring the sources of the Nile, let us look more closely at the rare texts which allude to a possible source.

In a hymn to 'The Lord of Eternity' we read,

O sole God who hast no equal,
Thou hast created them according to thy heart . . .
The mountainous countries, Syria, Sudan-Ethiopia
And the plain of Egypt . . .

Thou createst the Nile in the Dwat [Beyond] and bringest it forth at thy pleasure to give life to the people . . .
Thou makest every nation live, however distant it may be. Thou hast set a Nile in Heaven which descends for them and makes currents of water on the mountains like the great green (sea), watering their fields in their settlements.
How excellent are thy ways, O Lord of Eternity! A Nile in Heaven is the gift that thou hast made to the foreign countries, and to all the beasts of the mountain which walk upon foot, just like the Nile which comes from the Dwat for the Beloved Land [of Egypt].
(N. de G. Davis, *The Rock Tombs of El Amarna*, VI.)

It is literally true that the Nile has its sources in 'foreign countries': it collects the 'waters from heaven' which form rivers 'on the mountains', flowing from the icy summits of the Ruwenzori Range in Uganda and from the flanks of the active volcanoes of the Mufumbiro in Ruanda, to be joined by waters from Lake Victoria. Thus born from peaks of 'fire and ice' in the equatorial zone, and ceaselessly nourished by condensation throughout the seasonless year, the White Nile descends rapidly to Lake Albert, and from there broadens its girth to flow indolently through immense plateaux, forming the Bahr-el-Gebel (The Sea from the Mountains). There it is joined by the Bahr-el-Ghazel (Sea of Gazelles) forming a tropical, swampy region where all sorts of wild animals live.

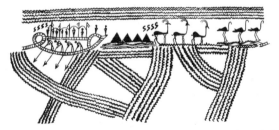

The paintings on certain prehistoric vases found in Egypt strikingly evoke the regions described above: men paddling in boats over innumerable watercourses whose banks are peopled with ibex and ostrich, outlined against a mountainous distance. It is interesting that not only do the majority of animals used in the later hieroglyphic writing come from these regions, but so, according to E.A. Wallis

Budge, do certain funerary customs; and of these, some come from Uganda. These analogies are due not to these tribes having borrowed from the Egyptians, he says, but to common African beliefs which have persisted in their essential forms from the Neolithic period to the present. For example, the notion of the 'double' associated with the birth of every child, so characteristic of Pharaonic belief, also exists in Uganda. And in the bas-reliefs at Der-el-Bahari and at Luxor, describing the divine births of Hatshepsut and of Amenophis III, it is a figure of the Nile that presents the newborn child and its double, the *ka*, to its father Amun-Rê.

In the Bahr-el-Gebel and the Bahr-el-Ghazel the White Nile loses more than half of its waters into the swamplands. In view of this limited flow, and the fact that the rainfall producing it is continuous rather than seasonal, the possibility that the White Nile is the source of the river's annual flood must be excluded. What then is the true cause of this remarkable event? This question intrigued the early Greek travellers, who tried very hard to learn the answer, the Egyptian priests still continuing to insist, even at this late period, that the Nile has two sources, one in Heaven and one in the Dwat, and that they both, contrary to all evidence, spring forth at Bigah. In fact there is only a single known line of hieroglyphic text which is on the right track. This is found in a text dating from the time of King Taharka (approximately 700 BC):

Now a marvellous thing happened in the time of His Majesty . . . When the time of the Nile's swelling arrived, it started to grow considerably each day; after a number of days had passed in which it grew each day, it inundated the mountains of the land of the South and the lowlands of the North. The country was similar to an inert primordial ocean, and the sand-shoals could not be distinguished from the river. Its flood had risen up to the city of Thebes.

Then His Majesty had the annals of the ancestors brought, to see what the Nile had done in their times, but nothing like this was found therein. It was a downpour from Heaven, in Nubia, that had made the mountains sparkle all the way to their boundaries. (Stela from the year 6 of King Taharka.)

The statement that it was 'a downpour from Heaven, in Nubia' that provoked the life-saving flood is perfectly correct, for in fact it is the torrential rains occurring in the high mountains of Ethiopia around Lake Tana which feed the Blue Nile and then provide the major part of the enormous flow of the flooding river. The smaller Sobet and Atbara rivers provide a secondary contribution. The actual cause of these rains at this precise point on the globe is a mystery, yet to be solved: research making use of artificial satellites is going on at the present time.

Our text also describes the countryside at the time of the inundation as being similar to an inert, primordial ocean. This expanse of water, extending for a length of more than 1000 kilometres (over 600 miles), and having a width of sometimes 10 or even 20 kilometres (up to 12 miles), has an absorbing beauty. It is a natural phenomenon which annually recalls the mystery of the Creation, when all existence suddenly emerged from the cosmic ocean by virtue of a single divine impulse.

Creation

The Four Centres of Instruction

How to describe the indescribable?
How to show the unshowable?
How to express the unutterable?
How to seize the ungraspable instant?
Before there was any opposition, any yes and no, positive and negative; before there was any complementarity, high and low, light and shadow; before there was presence or absence, life or death, heaven or earth: there was but one incomprehensible Power, alone, unique, inherent in the Nun, the indefinable cosmic sea, the infinite source of the Universe, outside of any notion of Space and Time. This vision of the original unity was common to every period and initiatory centre – Heliopolis, Memphis, Hermopolis and Thebes.

The great mystery is the passage from invisible into visible, to be realized by the Power which from the incomprehensible One will call forth the Many.

The first impulse is a projection of the inner desire of the Creator-to-be to know himself, to realize his own consciousness. This originating power is symbolized by the heart, and the act of projecting by an arm that throws, or the drawn bow about to let fly its arrow, or the boomerang which comes back after having reached its goal. The result is the Becoming, expressed hieroglyphically by the scarab, Khepri (see p. 14): this insect passes through three essential phases, egg, larva and nymph, before realizing its final winged form.

Vast notions such as these are suggested by the particular hieroglyphs used to word the stories related to the great mythic lines associated with each of the centres of instruction. Each of these lines emphasizes a different aspect of the cosmic cycle of Creation, Becoming and Return.

The oldest known religious texts, the so-called Pyramid Texts, are found in the burial chambers of the royal pyramids of the Fifth and Sixth Dynasties. Consisting of long vertical columns of hieroglyphs engraved into the stone walls, these inscriptions have the central purpose of facilitating the king's ascension into the heavens and his return to the side of his father, the Supreme God, where he will live eternally in the form of a pure and luminous spirit (*akh*).

The One, the Eternal, can be defined only through his countless qualities, which alone are nameable. These names then represent the active functional principles, the Neterw, cosmic or vital powers which find expression as the genesis of the world unfolds. Thus, through the invocations addressed to these powers – not gods but 'divine entities' or divine attributes – we can reconstitute the general outline of a cosmogony which was probably already very ancient by the time of the Pyramid Texts. This cosmogony is frequently recalled in the texts of all periods, but was never further developed.

Heliopolis
At Heliopolis the mystery of the Creation is described in its archetypal aspect. Here the name Atum is given to the One, the unique Power which will become the Creator or Demiurge. Atum means both All and Nothing, the potential totality of the Universe which is as yet unformed and intangible – for first Atum must 'project himself' or distinguish himself from the Nun, and thereby annihilate the Nun in its original inert state. 'Atum becomes.'

This first act is expressed in three major ways:

Hail Atum! Hail Khepri, he who becomes from himself!
You culminate in this your name of 'hill', you become in this your name of Scarab Khepri. (Pyramid Texts, 1587.)

Atum-Khepri, you culminate as hill, you raise yourself up as the Benu Bird from the ben-ben stone in the abode of the phoenix at Heliopolis. (Pyramid Texts, 1652.)

Atum surges out of the cosmic waters in the form of the primordial hill. He then 'spits out' (*ishish*) the first of the divine qualities or powers: Shu, the Principle of air and of space, symbolized by the feather he wears on his head. Atum then 'expectorates' (*tfnt*) the second Principle, the lion-headed Tefnut, who most probably represents the element of Fire.

In another version, 'Atum gives birth to himself through masturbation at Heliopolis', causing 'the seed from the kidneys to come' (Pyramid Texts, 1248). He then brings the twins Shu and Tefnut into the world.

In a third version, Atum creates himself by the projection of his own heart, and brings forth eight elementary principles which, together with himself, make up the Nine, the Great Ennead of Heliopolis: Shu and Tefnut, then Geb, the Earth, Nut, the Sky, and finally Osiris and Isis, Seth and Nepthys, entities of cyclic life and renewal, of death and rebirth. It is written that 'none of these entities is separate from him, Atum' (Pyramid Texts, 1655).

Thus by means of self-coagulation, or by his semen, or by the projection of his heart, Atum creates. The evocative images of the Pyramid Texts are further elucidated by a 'Coffin Text' from the Middle Kingdom (after 2040 BC) in which the dead person, who identifies himself with each of the divinities he evokes, says: 'I was the soul of Shu who is on the flame, the fire that Atum produced from his hand when he masturbated.' The male seed is here considered a catalyst, or in alchemical terms a 'styptic fire': a coagulating agent which causes the 'first earth' or 'primordial hill' to emerge from the undefined cosmic substance of the Nun. This initial condensing agent is symbolized by the spermatozoon which coagulates the female albuminous liquid exactly as the heat of a flame does the white of an egg. In addition, the mention of the 'soul' of Shu indicates that we are still in the realm of subtle elements, thus of abstraction.

Atum of Heliopolis is thus seen as the carrier of the invisible fire or seed, the cause – still metaphysical – of the first definition to arise from the undefined Nun. He then brings forth from himself the group of nine divine principles (eight of them plus himself) which will order the Becoming – the Great Ennead. In the Pyramid Texts this Great Ennead doubles, and then itself becomes a generative power. 'The King came forth from between the thighs of the divine Nine', or again 'from between the thighs of the two divine Nines', relating the number nine to generation.

The ancient Egyptians intuited a great deal from their understanding of the natural laws of numbers. It has been discovered only recently, with the aid of the electron microscope, that the spermatozoon is formed of a head and a long tail made up of nine threads. It is carrier of a centriole composed of nine (or multiples of nine) tubes, and these tubes direct the entire process of the division of the living cell, a division which is in fact a multiplication.

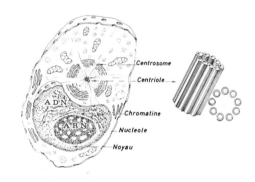

It is the action of the sperm that causes the female ovum to contract immediately after penetration and to form an englobing membrane, thereby prohibiting the access of any other sperm. The centrosome then divides and the centrioles are carried to the two poles of the ovum. There is contact between the two pronuclei, male and female: an impalpable instant, immediately followed by the division of the cell into two new cells, which will also in turn divide. This process of halving is at the basis of all Pharaonic mathematics, as is confirmed by the famous lines,

> I am One that transforms into Two
> I am Two that transforms into Four
> I am Four that transforms into Eight
> After this I am One.
> (Coffin of Petamon, Cairo Museum no. 1160.)

The eternal mystery then is the passage from One to Two, the first scission of the initial Unity, which has the immediate consequence of a polarization. This polarization defines two antithetical forces, positive and negative, which in Pharaonic myth are symbolized by Horus and Seth.

Memphis
In the myth originating at Memphis, Creation is taken one stage further in the direction of matter. Ptah (the Greek Hephaistos), the divine blacksmith, himself becomes the primordial fire and gives it substance. The archetypes *enunciated* by Atum at Heliopolis are here *materialized* by Ptah. The famous Shabaka Text (c. 710 BC) enumerates Ptah's eight hypostases or qualities as 'the Neterw who have come into existence in Ptah'. Ptah thus himself incarnates the primordial Eight, and then becomes Tatenenn, 'the earth which rises up', an evocation of the primordial hill. The same text continues, 'He who manifested himself as heart, he who manifested himself as tongue, in the likeness of Atum, is Ptah, the very ancient, who gave life to all the Neterw.' The heart and the tongue 'have power over' all the other members, since the tongue describes what the heart conceives. Thus Ptah re-creates the Great Ennead, and gives rise to all the qualities of things, through the Desire of his heart and the Word of his tongue.

It is said that the Ennead, which was the 'seed and hand of Atum', becomes the 'teeth and lips of Ptah' and gives a name to each thing, bringing it into existence. Divine principles and qualities (the Ennead) can now 'enter into all the species of things' – mineral, plant or animal – and become manifest through them. This is clearly an account of Creation by the Word.

Ptah, together with Sekhmet, the redoubtable lioness, whose name means 'the powerful', and Nefertum, 'the accomplishment of Atum', constitutes the first causal triad.

Hermopolis

From Hermopolis, city of Hermes (Thoth), Master of Writing, Numbers, Measurement and Time, comes the description of the Nun, the primordial environment, picturing its qualities and characteristics: 'He [the Demiurge] created the Eight. He formed its body as that of a sacred child who issues forth from a lotus in the middle of the Nun.'

The primordial Eight, as envisaged at Hermopolis (the Ogdoad), together form, as the text indicates, a single entity. The Nun is envisaged as a swampy mire, a seething primal cradle in which live four couples of serpents and frogs. Their names are Naun and Naunet, meaning both 'the initial waters' and 'inertia', Heh and Hehet, meaning 'spatial infinity'; Kek and Keket, 'the darkness'; and Amun and Amunet, 'That which is hidden'. This latter couple is sometimes replaced by Niau and Niaut, 'the void'.

As might be suspected, these qualities of the primordial state have often been compared with the shadowy waters of the Biblical Genesis, when 'the earth was without form and void, and darkness was upon the face of the deep'. But rather than regard the Nun as an initial or primal chaos, in the Biblical mode, it seems more fruitful to see it as indefinable substance, the eternal and infinite source of the Universe. The lotus, which has its roots in mud, its stem in water and its leaves and flowers opening out into air, receiving the celestial dew and the sun's rays, has always been a symbol of the four elements. This symbol is employed often in Egypt, in architecture as well as in myth. It appears in many legends of the Creation, including this very explicit one in which the Eight also figure:

You [the Eight] have made from your seed a germ [*bnn*], and you have instilled this seed in the lotus, by pouring the seminal fluid; you have deposited in the Nun, condensed into a single form, and your inheritor takes his radiant birth under the aspect of a child. (Edfu VI, 11–12, and Esna V, 263.)

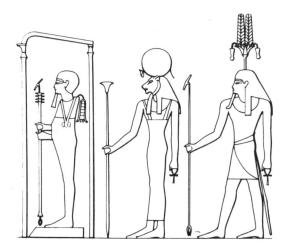

The Eight are called the 'fathers and mothers of Rê', for the child that comes forth from this primordial lotus is Rê, or Ra, the principle of light itself.

It is often said that Rê is himself the sun, which is inaccurate, for many texts affirm that Rê 'penetrates' the solar globe and causes it to shine, so that he renders it luminous by his passage. Thus Rê is not the light but that which provokes the phenomenon of light:

> I am he who made heaven and earth, formed the mountains and created what is above.
> I am he who made the water and created the celestial waves ...
> I am he who made the bull for the cow ...
> I am he who made the sky and the mysteries of the two horizons, I placed there the souls of the gods.
> I am he who opens his eyes, thus the light comes forth.
> I am he who closes his eyes, thus comes forth obscurity;
> On the order of whom the Nile's flood flows abroad, whose name is not known by the gods.
> I am he who made the hours, thus the days were born.
> I am he who opened the New Year's festival, who created the river.
> I am he who made the living fire ...
> I am Khepri in the morning, Rê at his noontide, Atum in the evening.

Thus Rê is all. He is called Atum-Rê at Heliopolis, Rê-Hor-Akhty at Memphis, and Amun-Rê at Thebes.

Thebes
The Theban myths present many features that perplex the modern scholar but did not seem to cause the ancient theologians the slightest distress.

To begin with, how is one to translate Apet-Sut, the name of the group of temples at Karnak, consecrated to the Theban Triad, Amun, Mut and Khonsu? We know that *sut* means 'place', and that *apet* designates the female hippopotamus, whose enormous belly symbolizes the gestating womb (see figure at left).

This word *apet* or *ipet* derives from the root *ip*, meaning 'to count' or 'to enumerate'. Apet-Sut can thus be translated as 'enumerator of the places', yet this still leaves one wondering why gestation is identified with the fact of counting.

How, furthermore, is one to explain the fact that the Great Ennead, composed of nine entities at Heliopolis and Memphis, is replaced by fifteen at Karnak?

How to explain the extraordinary advance of Amun, in Theban records dating from around the year 2000 BC, to the highest rank? Prior to this time he had been, with his counterpart Amonet, only one of the couples of the Hermopolitan Eight. Why at this moment does Amun (the Hidden), whose sacred animal is the ram, completely supplant the older Mentu, whose sacred animal is the bull? The answer to this question is made evident by the Precession of the Equinoxes – it was at this time that the position of the sun at the Spring Equinox moved from Taurus to Aries – except that it has never yet been generally acknowledged that the ancient Egyptians were familiar with this cycle. It is interesting, in this regard, that before the Taurean era of 4200–2100 BC, during which the cult of the bull Mentu was dominant – that is to say, during the predynastic period – the Spring Equinox was in the sign of Gemini (the Twins), and there was a dual monarchy in Egypt, each part of which had a double capital: Dep and Pe in the Kingdom of the North, and Nekhen and Nekheb in the Kingdom of the South. This theme of duality, also prominent in a number of sculpted tablets dating from that period, is further confirmed by the prototype of Hermes' staff, the caduceus with its twin serpents, several examples of which, engraved in gold leaf on the handles of flint knives, have been found, among other places, at El-Amrah.

The Theban myth, in attempting to clarify the relation between the mythic developments associated with Thebes, poses a further problem. The narrative runs as follows:

At the origin of time, there existed a serpent, Kam-at-f, 'he who has accomplished his time'. As his name indicates, this serpent ceased to exist when his time was past. He had, however, a son, Ir-ta, 'Creator of the Earth'. Ir-ta continued the work of his father and created the Eight Primordials of Hermopolis, among whom of course we find Amun, who declares *himself* to be the initial serpent, and

Amonet. The genealogy is presented as follows, in terms of four generations:

I. The serpent Kam-at-f, assimilated to Amun-Rê of Karnak.
II. The serpent Ir-ta, assimilated to Min-Amun of Luxor.
III. The Eight Primordials, one of whom is Amun, who thus re-generates himself.
IV. The solar child who comes forth from the lotus at Hermopolis, in other words Rê, product of the Eight Primordials, and also assimilated to Amun.

To make sense of this as a story, it would seem necessary to postulate, in defiance of our logic, that the future is anterior to the past, and that a being can be his own grandfather; or else we must give up trying to schematize and look for the real mystery – and the real coherence – hidden under the images. For it is unthinkable that the ancients would have covered the walls of their temples with such magnificent representations – sculpted with the utmost care – to express only absurdities. Nevertheless, such a conclusion seemed inescapable to many historians only a few decades ago. They viewed the past of humanity in terms of linear evolution, and became the prisoners of their own assumptions. Today, however, owing to new discoveries in many fields, we are beginning to witness a change in perspective, enabling fresh penetration into the ancient myths.

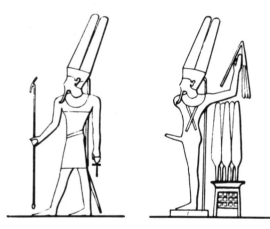

Thus, rather than try to distinguish between, say, an 'Amun of Karnak' and a 'Min-Amun of Luxor', we can see these entities as *hypostases,* the qualities or manifestations of the same indefinable principle: 'he whose name is hidden'. The Supreme Being under the name of Amun, represented in writing by a figure in walking position, is 'the vital breath which lives in all things', whereas under that of Amun-Rê he expresses particularly the solar aspect. Again, as Min-Amun, represented standing, ithyphallic and mummified, his arms raised with his sceptre and his high plumes which often cut through the sky, he seems to capture the celestial energy. This undoubtedly explains the red ribbon which encircles his forehead and trails on the ground. In the Temple of Medinet Habu, the inscriptions which accompany the representation of the procession of Min-Amun call him 'he who is above the clouds', or 'he who opens the clouds' – revealing his relation to rain, which, in Egypt, is principally due to thunderstorms. Thus there are serious reasons to believe (as G. A. Wainwright suggests) that the emblem of Min, which is of prehistoric origin, actually represents the thunderbolt. Whatever its variations, this symbol always expresses two opposing currents:

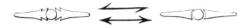

Later on, the thunderbolt, symbolized by arrows or other projectiles, became the attribute of the sky god Zeus-Jupiter-Amun.

Finally, under the name of 'bull of his mother', Min-Amun represents the inseminator *par excellence* in a permanent aspect; under the complex designation of Min-Amun-Bull-of-his-Mother he summarizes all the preceding qualities. He draws without cease from the infinite cosmic source of the Nun, and consequently has a feminine, nourishing aspect as well as the virile, procreative character.

There is similarly a coherent idea behind that curious name given to the Theban temples, Apet-Sut, 'enumerator of the places': each temple is consecrated to a particular entity or Neter, who is not a god but a principle, a mode of action of the Supreme Being. These Neterw then express the causes of phenomena, order the affinities or concordances between things, and give rise to their forms and 'signatures' (qualities). In other words, the Neterw preside over the modes and varieties which are revealed by number.

The Pythagorean axiom 'All is Number' was long considered an unrealistic proposition, until it was discovered that the properties of any given chemical element are governed by a specific whole number: the atomic number, corresponding to the number of protons and electrons belonging to its atom, as well as their distribution on the orbits (levels of energy) surrounding the nucleus. Hydrogen, for example, has an atomic number of 1, with only one electron in orbit, while helium has the number 2 and two electrons.

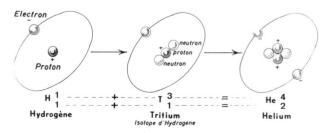

The transmutation of hydrogen into helium is at the origin of the birth of stars and, in our small world, provides the solar energy from which we benefit. Now if we are to believe the above schema, it must be acknowledged that the simplest possible nucleus, having a value of One, becomes triple in order to produce, in addition to itself, the second element having the atomic number Two. Here, then, matter itself expresses the mystery of becoming in terms of number: One into Two, the mystery which is at the very basis of all 'revelatory' teachings.

This suggests why the Pythagoreans placed number at the origin of all things. So great was their reverence that they swore their oath on the divine tetractys, or sacred triangle, established quite simply on the natural sequence of numbers, $1+2+3+4=10$:

– nine strokes grouped around the incomprehensible One. This originating triangle is illustrated by the Great Ennead of Heliopolis.

Similarly, the unexpected switch from nine to fifteen entities or hypostases of Amun-Rê in his temple at Karnak, Thebes, reflects the pentactys:

– twelve strokes encircling the divine creative triangle, and representing this triangle manifested.

One can already sense from these considerations the role of numbers as generative powers, and thus their relation to the names of the Theban sanctuaries. There exists, however, a still more striking demonstration of this relation: a hymn consecrated to Amun-Rê, constructed on a series of plays on words and on numbers. This hymn (Leyden Papyrus I, 350) is composed of twenty-seven stanzas, numbered with the first nine numbers, then with the nine tens, then with nine hundreds (see p. 78).

The particular character of each stanza is determined by the implications associated with its number. A stanza beginning with One contains an evocation of the 'First Time', the Creation, and associates Thebes with that event. The great temple of Amun itself is said to be 'the place of origin and outlet of the Nun', clearly alluding once more to the primordial hill and therefore to the beginning of all generation or creative enumeration. Thebes is said to be more exact, or 'more enumerated', than any other city.

The stanzas beginning with the number Two give examples of the dual principle, such as the 'double

horizon'. A distinction is also made between the two principal divisions of the aspects of our being: the subtle body which is immortal, and the gross body which must undergo cycles of death and rebirth.

One of the stanzas beginning with Three alludes to a 'third' element arising from the collision of two opposing forces, using the thunderbolt as an example. It is in this stanza that we find the famous passage of theological synthesis:

Three gods are all the gods: Amun, Rê, Ptah, who have no equal. 'He whose name is hidden' is Amun, whose countenance is Rê and whose body is Ptah. Their cities on earth, established in perpetuity, are Thebes, Heliopolis, Memphis, for eternity. Amun-Rê-Ptah, Unity-Trinity.

Myth and magic

Let us call Spirit pure energy – but it is known to us only as polarized energy.
Let us call God consciousness – but it is known to us only through complementation.
Let us call Light the first phenomenon – but it is known to us only through darkness.
Let us call the Original Scission the first act of Becoming – but it is known to us only as separation. (R.A.Schwaller de Lubicz, Le Temple de l'homme, III, 388.)

From the moment the One 'regards himself', there are 'He and the Other', the two opposites. These two will take on many names, each one corresponding to the distinctive character of a given moment in any of the manifestations of life. Confronting order and harmony there will inevitably be disorder and disharmony; this is a necessity inherent in all creation, in which nothing can exist without its inverse.

Confronting the Eye of Horus, symbol of Light and of man's ultimate spiritual quest, are the testicles of Seth, symbolizing the causes of revolt, violence and turbulence. Seth and Horus are the eternal antagonists. Confronting the cosmic equilibrium of Rê is Apophi, the monstrous flint-breasted serpent which is responsible for such violent perturbations as drought, earthquakes, thunderstorms, tempests and hailstorms, which only Seth, armed with similar phenomena, is capable of countering.

The Pyramid Texts repetitively evoke and attempt to activate all these Powers which govern and assure the life of the Universe; and yet it is useless to search in these incantations for an orderly cosmogony in the form of a narrated train of events. Just one 'magical papyrus' from the Late Period (about 300 BC) unites the principal notions of the Creation, contained in the Pyramid Texts, into a relatively coherent whole. This incantation, used to avoid or minimize the catastrophes brought on by Apophi, sets out to reinforce the natural order of things by recalling the different phases of the Creation. The Supreme Being, called

Atum at Heliopolis, here takes the name of Rê, the Principle of Light. The papyrus has the title Book of Knowing the Modes of Existence of Rê and of Overthrowing the Serpent Apophi.

The entire incantation is repeated twice in two slightly different forms. In both versions the reciter identifies himself with the Demiurge. In the longer of them, the Introduction is largely composed of modulations of words all constructed on the same root. The continual repetition of the same phonemes gives it a compelling quality, rather like the Hindu *mantram*.

For example, in hieroglyphic writing the sacred scarab *kheper* represents a word designating this insect itself, but also all the metamorphoses or transformations of which it is the symbol, as well as the idea of 'becoming' in general. The word *kheper* thus means 'to become' in all possible verbal forms, while Khepri is the entity embodied in the sun as it rises in the morning, when darkness becomes light.

The effect of this strange composition can be better understood by looking at its opening statement written phonetically:

Thus spoke the Lord of All:
kheper-i   kheper kheper   kheperu   m kheperu
[when] I became, the becoming became, I have become in becoming [the form]
n Khepri   kheper   m   sep tepy –
of Khepri who came into being on the First Time –

and the text continues: 'when I became, the transformations became, all the metamorphoses [*kheperu*] coming to pass after I had become.'

Next comes a long dissertation on the anteriority of the Supreme Being, in which he declares several times that he was alone in the Nun before the Creation and that it was he who created the primordial entities. And yet he says:

> I did all that I desired in this [nonexistent!] world,
> I dilated myself in it.
> I contracted my own hand, all alone, before there was any birth.
> My own mouth came to me and Magic was my name.

First we find desire, expressed with one of the forms of the verb to love (*mr*), symbolizing affinity, attraction. Then dilation (*usekh*), immediately followed by contraction (*ths*): inhalation, exhalation, diastole, systole, the first pulsation of life, the heartbeat. Thus existence begins, thus commences the play of alternation, enabling genesis to proceed.

Then his mouth, the means of expression of the word (*hu*), 'comes to him', giving birth to magic (*heka*); these are two fundamental qualities of the Supreme Being which we shall encounter again, along with *sia* (knowledge), when we come to discuss the cycle of day and night.

After enunciating these essential functions the text continues:

Many were the metamorphoses which came from my mouth before the Sky had become, before the earth had come into being, before any ground or reptile was created in these places.

As in the Heliopolitan myth, this represents the metaphysical phase of Creation, the enunciation of archetypes. For the full realization of the mystery of the Origin, a further concretizing power must be called upon. This power takes a different name and aspect in each of the initiatic centres, and in the present instance it is seen as the *ba*, one of the subtle elements in the makeup of human (and other personified) beings. The *ba* has been called the 'soul'; yet this concept is much too confined; the *ba* serves here as the abstract coagulative agent – the determining, individualizing force which, acting as a catalyst, provokes the first 'specification'.

I made therein the modes of metamorphosis starting from this my *ba*. I coagulated [*ths*] among them, in the Nun, in the Inertia, at the time when I had not yet found any place where I could raise myself up.

Here again is the external mystery of the first coagulation, the inexplicable 'becoming' through which, from the original non-polarized Energy, the 'primordial hill' or mound, symbolizing mass, emerges as the first concrete object. The Supreme Being first 'meditates' this original 'something', and the projection of his thought puts into action another notion which is also untranslatable: *akh*.

Another of the subtle parts of Being, *akh* plays a considerable role in the sacred language. *Akh* is a state, a quality, and an activity, signifying the spirit; radiant, transcendent light; and transfiguration by this light. *Akh* is at the origin and at the end of all vital experience of becoming conscious. Thus *akh* as a verb cannot be accurately defined. Some scholars propose 'to think', others 'to be efficacious', but 'to idealize', or 'to irradiate' or 'to illuminate' could equally be suggested, remembering always that it is a question of Spirit, of abstraction.

That which I illuminated in my heart [was] the plan [of the universe] which presented itself to me, I made every creature when I was alone. I planned in my heart, I created other metamorphoses, very many were the transformations of Khepri [and] the children became, in the forms of their progenitors …

These last lines would have us believe that the phase of procreation had begun; but the incantation continues:

It is I who spat out [*ishsh*] Shu, I who expectorated [*tfn*] Tefnut. I had come into being as One God, and behold there were Three. Two entities had come into this world. Shu and Tefnut rejoiced in the Nun, in which they were.

The first mystery is thus realized: One has become Three. And with this creative trinity the process of genesis should be able to commence. Curiously enough, in the magical text there is none of this, but only this same passage written three times. Furthermore, before each repetition further problematic events are recounted. Why, for example, a moment after Shu and Tefnut have been created, do they go away into the immensity for an 'aeonic' length of time? – and why is it that the Divine Eye pursues them?

My Eye was behind them during the aeons that they passed far away from me.

Variant:

It was my Eye that brought them back to me after the aeons that they stayed far away from me.

In attempting to understand these passages it may be helpful to draw a parallel between this mythic structure and a more formal outline of basic philosophical ideas – R.A.Schwaller de Lubicz's formulation of the 'irreducible magnitudes', that is, the sequence of notions that are fundamental and necessary in any conception of the Universe. Let us consider them as they (in his words) 'engender themselves, in their septuple order':

Abstract Series
Origin · Time · Movement · $\left\{\begin{array}{l}\text{Pathway}\\\text{Space}\\\text{Volume}\end{array}\right\}$ · Force · Energy · Mass
Concrete Series

In Egyptian terms, Origin corresponds to the Demiurge, alone in the Nun; Mass, the last and lowest term, corresponds to the primordial hill. Midway between these two extremes we find Space, which has the double nature of pathway and volume. Now, the entity who is said to hold up the sky and separate it from the earth is Shu. He undoubtedly represents Space, but the role of his female counterpart, Tefnut, has remained undetermined: so much so that some scholars see her as Humidity and others as Fire. The schema above enables us to suggest that these twins both represent Space, in its dual aspect: Space as Pathway in the 'Abstract Series' and Space as Volume in the 'Concrete Series'.

Between Origin and Space as Pathway we necessarily have the notions of Time and Movement. These seem to be illustrated by the journey of Shu and Tefnut, since it lasted 'aeons', and naturally implies a path. Furthermore, as we shall see shortly, the travelling Eye has its own relationship with Time and with Volume.

The incantation then continues:

I brought together my members, they issued from me myself. After I produced excitation with my fist, my desire was realized by my hand. The seed fell from my mouth. I spat out Shu, I expectorated Tefnut. Whereas I was One, now I am Three.

This passage is particularly startling, for while the Pyramid Texts seem to be speaking of an ordinary emission of semen, here the seed rises up and is expelled through the mouth, an unmistakable reference to the principle of elevation and subtilization.

Furthermore, as part of its biological function, in provoking the polarization of the ovum's doubled centrosome, the spermatozoon activates an attracting force which acts on the chromosomes, thus manifesting an energy. Likewise in physics, when a mass is subject to a force, energy is produced.

Thus the entire 'Concrete Series' of the schema is brought into play by the different images of this magical text; and the strange metaphors it uses to express creation can bear transposition into modern philosophic and scientific terms – although the text certainly has implications on other levels as well.

The tale continues. Once more the twins go away and the Eye goes after them; and once more, for the third time, the Demiurge creates the dual aspect of space, and the twins depart for an 'aeonic' time. Then, after a section in which the papyrus is damaged – to the frustration of its translators, for this part seems to be dealing with the 'root of the Eye' – there follows a little story which is impossible to pass over in silence, although its meaning remains obscure. While the Neterw or divine entities, as we have seen, come from the Creator's mouth (his saliva or his word), man is created from his eye. It is said that the Creator wept, and from his tears (*rmyt*) humanity (*rmtt*) was born. The coming into existence of man is explained solely by this play on words:

Shu and Tefnut brought back my Eye behind them after I had reassembled my members. I *wept* over them and it is thus that *humanity* came into existence.

But,

The Eye became enraged when it returned, for it found that another had grown in its place, and that it had been replaced by 'the sparkling' [*akh*].

The fury of the Eye vanished, however, when the Creator placed it on his forehead in the place occupied by the *uraeus* (the raised cobra), and to this day it terrorizes all assailants, repulses all enemies, and 'governs the entire earth', for it is said that 'it took root'.

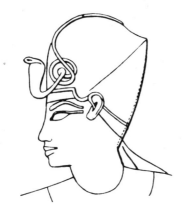

Only now does the process of Creation begin:

Shu and Tefnut engendered Geb and Nut [Earth and Sky]. Geb and Nut gave birth to Osiris, Horus-Khenty-irty, Seth, then Isis and Nepthys, of their bodies, one after the other . . . and they gave birth to the multitudes of this world.' (Bremner-Rhind Papyrus 27, 1 and 28, 26.)

The misadventures of the travelling Eye may seem peculiar to anyone unaware of the myths relating to the eyes, which play a large role in all Pharaonic symbolism. The Eyes of the Supreme Being are the symbols of light, the twin luminaries of the sky: 'The right Eye of the Supreme Being is the Sun and his left Eye is the Moon.' The right Eye is the visible sun which gives light and vitalizing heat – but also the fire that burns. It is important to note that, although represented two-dimensionally in the bas-reliefs as a disc, the sun was recognized to be a globe, just as the eye itself is spherical.

Man has forever been captivated by the moon and its phases. Its monthly disappearance, its waxing and waning, have been the subject of innumerable legends which in Egypt all relate to the left Eye. The best known of these fables is that of the Eye of Horus which is wounded by his eternal antagonist Seth. Thoth, Master of Writing, the Sciences and of Time, whose sacred animals are the ibis and the baboon, most often takes the role of separating the two combatants. The hurt eye must be healed and its parts gathered together; and this task is also accomplished by Thoth, who thus forms the Oudja (or 'whole, healthy') Eye.

 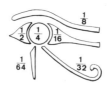

Egyptian arithmetic was based on dimidiation – halving – rather than on addition, and the eye plays a part in the notation. The *hekat*, the unit of volume used in the measurement of grain, is represented graphically by the Oudja Eye, and its fractions by the individual strokes of the glyph.

Thus the lunar Eye is at the basis of the measurement of both time, because of the lunation which defines the month, and volume, because of its fractioning. It is interesting to recall that while vision through one eye is sufficient for the perception of distance, it is only when the ocular axes of both eyes converge that we are able to form the notion of three-dimensional space and therefore of volume.

The Egyptians also had an explanation for the moon's light, 'the light of the night, the left Eye . . . which rises in the East, while the globe of the sun is in the West' (implying that the moon reflects the sun's light). It is also written that the moon is invisible when it is too close to the sun. In other words, at the time of its conjunction with the sun (new moon), the moon is invisible, and at the moment of opposition (full moon) it is the mirror of the sun. Appropriately, the Egyptians often fashioned hand mirrors in the form of a slightly flattened disc with an image of an eye in the centre. The handle represents the *ouadj*, papyrus plant, symbol of the widening of the heart.

Irrespective of all the quasi-scientific explanations, based on the phases of the moon, that may be offered, the myth of the Eye of Horus, recovered after being torn out by Seth, remains elusive. This Eye symbolizes the divine light imprisoned in matter, which must be liberated. Thus it is said that the Eye is the seat of the soul and is all-powerful, for its possesses in itself the means for this deliverance.

Through the crossing of the nerve fibres in the optic chiasma, the left half of the brain sees with the right eye and the right half with the left eye. This interweaving of perceptions renders us conscious of objects and of their forms. Thus the Eye is related in Egyptian thought to the divinities of weaving, to *sia*, knowledge, and to Sia, the divinity of knowledge, whose name is written hiero-glyphically as a piece of cloth, because the eye, our predominant means of gaining knowledge, shares the principle of crossing by which a fabric is made.

Yet even the enrichment we call knowledge must be 'sublimated' and taken to a higher level, for purely cerebral knowledge is as mortal as the instrument, *ais*, the brain, by which it is acquired. Is it then for the sake of this 'sublimation' that the Enraged Eye intervenes – the third eye, which the Creator placed on his forehead and which takes the form of a cobra poised to strike? This is the Eye that became all-powerful at the moment it 'took root'.

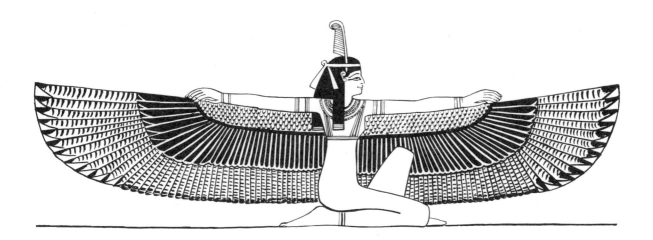

Among certain lizards, the Lacertians (some of which inhabit the Nile Valley), there is an actual third eye, 'rooted' to the pineal body, which is situated just behind the 'optic layers' below the cerebral cortex. Little is known even today about the pineal body and its functions. Certain authors around the time of Galen (AD 131–201) felt that 'it must serve as a sluice-gate regulating the quantity of spirit necessary to maintain psychic equilibrium'.

This spirit, the transcendental spiritual light which was called *akh* by the ancient Egyptians, would require an entire volume for the description of its qualities. However, a strange passage in the Pyramid Texts tells us that the King 'absorbed the seven frontal cobras [*uraei*] which then became the seven cervical vertebrae which commanded the entire dorsal spine'. These cobras, which spit fire, recall the Kundalini 'serpent-fire' of the Hindu tradition, and this passage also seems to refer to certain of the vital centres or chakras, one of which occupies precisely the place of the royal *uraeus* in the forehead.

Thus the Eye evokes the means of the perception of light in all its forms, from the physical light of the sun and moon to the light of knowledge, and to the inner illumination of the awakened Spirit. And the *uraeus* is the magnificent symbol of all the powers related to this triple conception.

Becoming

There is a fundamental notion, abstract yet vitally real, which colours all the myth, the morality and the life of the ancient Egyptians. This is Maât. Divine entities and human beings alike live 'by Maât, in Maât and for Maât'.

This single name expresses all notions of equilibrium and poise – an image of Maât is pictured above. The scales, and Maât's symbol, the feather, support a plumb line at the end of which hangs the plumb bob. Maât represents therefore accuracy, honesty, fairness, faithfulness, rectitude, and in this aspect becomes the emblem of the judge, who in the late period wore a small Maât of lapis lazuli on his breast. Maât is the symbol of Justice and Truth, of authenticity, legitimacy, integrity, legality.

Maât is also the symbol of harmony, in the sense of accurate tones and perfect musical accords. In the New Kingdom (after 1567 BC) harps are often decorated with a figurine of Maât.

The principle of Harmony is a cosmic law, the Voice of God. Whatever be the disorder that man or fortuitous natural accident may provoke, Nature, left to herself, will put everything in order again through affinities (the Consciousness in all things). Harmony is the a priori Law written in all of Nature; it imposes itself on our intelligence, yet it is in itself incomprehensible. (R. A. Schwaller de Lubicz, *Le Roi de la théocratie pharaonique*.)

Thus Maât does not judge: she is consciousness itself, and also the individual consciousness that each person carries in his heart, for she is both the motivating force and the goal of life. She is invoked on all occasions; she is omnipresent. Maât moves and directs existence, and Maât is its ultimate treasure.

This profound awareness of equilibrium and harmony gave the Egyptian people and their leaders a wholesome and pure moral sense, as the early visitors to Egypt attested. This same awareness is the sole explanation of the marvels of their craftsmanship, indisputable records of a need for perfection, a taste and refinement, that remained undiminished over nearly three thousand years.

Maât in its widest sense is Cosmic Consciousness, the rightness and order which have reigned since the beginning of things: 'When the heavens were sleeping [= inert, unconscious state], I lived with my daughter Maât, one within me, the other around me', says the Demiurge (Coffin Texts, I, spell 80), revealing the meaning of a phrase found in some texts, 'the double Maât': individual consciousness and Cosmic Consciousness.

A similar text further says, that when, before the Creation, Atum the Demiurge wished that his heart might live,

Nun said to Atum: Breathe in thy daughter Maât, bring her to thy nose in order that thy heart may live. That she be not removed from thee, that thy daughter Maât be with thy son Shu whose name is Life.

Thus even before the Creation the awakening of Consciousness (Maât) provokes the first breath (Shu) issuing from the nostrils of the Creator. It is Shu who sustains life, causes the heart to beat and the lungs to breathe, and who, in one myth, brings forth the initial egg at the origin of time.

All the images describing the first creative act express the same two notions of an indescribable origin – God as indivisible Unity or non-polarized energy, and God as Creator, polarized energy, Unity conscious of itself. In *Le Temple de l'homme* (I, 61), R.A. Schwaller de Lubicz concludes:

The Universe is nothing but Consciousness, and in all its appearances reveals nothing but an evolution of Consciousness, from its origin to its end, which is a return to its cause. It is the goal of every 'initiatory' religion to teach the way to this ultimate union.

The Egyptian mind

Pharaonic Egyptian art and symbolism presents, at least on the surface, a number of contrasting and apparently contradictory features.

Thus, the artistic figurations depicting daily life, particularly those in the tombs of the noblemen of all periods, display an extraordinarily lively and accurate sense of observation, with a preference for positive and logical sequences of events. Certain tableaux, such as those of fishing, or the playful scuffles of young men in skiffs, or of boat construction and other crafts, give a virtually cinematic impression which shows each essential movement and gesture of the action depicted. Similarly, the secular literature, the tales and proverbs, are expressed in picturesque language, and reveal a clear and sound form of thinking. On the other hand, as we have seen, the theology seems continually to challenge our rational logic, often presenting side by side two notions which seem difficult to reconcile, if not contradictory.

On closer study, this inconsistency starts to disappear, for one begins to discover certain essential characteristics of the ancients' way of thinking which determined the formulation of both their written and figured works.

First of all, the ancient Egyptian mind nearly always envisages a notion together with its inverse, which is indissociable from it.

For example, dilation is inconceivable without contraction; likewise every concrete object necessarily has two sides. This leads to the notion of reciprocity, in which an activity in one direction implies an activity in the other. This is continually pointed out, for example in the formula from the daily temple ritual, 'Thy purification is the purification of Horus and vice versa.'

Secondly, the sense of 'crossing' is of capital importance – as in the symbolism of the Eye and of Sia, knowledge (see p. 16). We meet this very same idea again in one of the earliest symbols, that of Neith, the Greek Athena, which consists of two crossed arrows in front of a shield. Neith is the divinity both of weaving and of intelligence. 'Knowledge' or 'science' consists in the crossing of the warp and weft. This image clearly evokes the fact that all data recorded in the brain results from the intercrossing of sensations perceived by means of our sense organs, just as the threads are crossed in weaving.

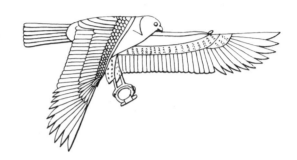

A third characteristic of the Pharaonic mentality is an appreciation of simultaneity. This is expressed in various ritual representations – encountered chiefly in the temples – by the superimposition in a single image of several points of view and moments of time. The falcon hovering over the king is a typical example: its head is in profile; one of its wings is represented as seen from above; the other wing and the tail are seen from below. What at first seems to be a frozen moment of flight thus actually represents several moments of flight seen together.

Another example is provided by the calendrical system of the ancient Egyptians. This system is comparable to no other, for it is neither exclusively stellar nor solar nor lunar nor seasonal, but incorporates all these cycles in a simultaneity which seems inconceivable to us (see p. 75).

Likewise, in viewing the myths, it is necessary to consider all the symbolic aspects and images simultaneously, and not to fall into the trap of trying at any cost to find a *single* line of chronology or logical sequence.

The Egyptian ability to maintain simultaneously two apparently divergent points of view is revealed by the so-called opposition between polytheism and monotheism in Pharaonic religion. There are two categories of names given to the Neterw, the divine entities, at various centres of instruction. Names in the first group represent qualities, functions or transitory states: Nefertum, Accomplishment of Atum; Sekhmet, the Powerful; Hathor, House of Horus; Mut, Mother. Those in the second group imply absoluteness, and therefore uniqueness: Amun, the Hidden; Atum, All-or-Nothing. In fact, these categories, and those of unity and multiplicity, coexist in Egyptian thought – just as we have learned from quantum physics to see that light-as-waves and light-as-particles are simultaneously true. In popular maxims 'God' is one:

If a man is eminent and respected it is God who has made him wise.

To be generous is a gift of God, but he who listens to his belly belongs to the enemy. (Instructions of Ptahhotep, Fifth Dynasty, about 2450 BC.)

Worship God and do not say 'This is discouraging!' Do not let your arms drop, but act with sprightliness.'

If morality was based on a monotheistic sanction, then popular belief would seem to have been essentially monotheistic.

In the famous Chapter 17 of the Book of the Dead (or Book of the Coming Forth into Day), known for its commentaries provided by the scribe himself, it is stated that the Creator came into existence from himself when he rose up from the primordial cosmic ocean, and that all the divinities following him came into existence when he pronounced the names of his own members. It is impossible to avoid the conclusion that these innumerable entities all participate in the One, and are but its qualities or hypostases. It is for this reason that the deceased can identify himself successively with each of the entities he evokes, finally maintaining that he is the Supreme Being himself.

Eternity and perpetuity

Two concepts which clearly appear at the basis of the cosmogonies we have tried to bring together here, at first glance seem contradictory.

On the one hand there is the notion of a 'constant and ceaseless Becoming', without beginning or end, attested to in the structure of the language itself by certain grammatical peculiarities, and in the religious literature by the frequent affirmation of an 'eternity' which seems to be beyond all Time.

On the other hand, the texts also speak of 'before' the Creation, thus implying the notion of a fixed beginning, and consequently of an end. Many texts indeed refer to 'the First Time', or insist on 'primordial entities' confirming the idea of an origin situated in time – just as, conversely, the following lines imply an 'end':

> All that has been created will return into the Nun ...
> Myself alone, I persist, unknown, invisible to all.

'I', the Supreme Being who has no name.

This small phrase contains a resolution of the problem posed by expressing a certitude in the eternity of the absolute Being who is commingled with the Nun, the infinite cosmic source from which everything comes and into which everything is ultimately resolved. At the same time it alludes to the transitory character of every creature, subject to a beginning and an end.

Thus the contradiction is in fact only apparent, for it corresponds to the double aspect of eternity as conceived by the ancients and which they transcribed by the two distinct words, *nhh* and *djt*, translated by 'eternity' and 'perpetuity'. This double aspect of eternity has been particularly studied by Jan Assmann in his book *Zeit und Ewigkeit im alten Ägypten*. Assmann says that the Creation represents, not a struggle between Chaos and Order, but the constant transformation of One into Many. The eternal is the cosmic energy which replenishes the world, constantly giving it life and sustenance. This is eternity in its absolute and permanent sense, outside of all time. Parallel to this is the notion of 'perpetuity' and continuity: life is threatened by periodic crises which the temple ritual works magically to keep at bay. Our notion of time is born from this periodicity, and from the cyclic character of all cosmic life.

The Pharaonic texts accordingly proclaim, on the one hand, the immutability of the Supreme Being and, on the other, the cyclic nature of death and rebirth, expressed in the myths as perpetual renewal. The sun is reborn each year at the winter solstice, after the shortest day. The moon is reborn each month after new moon. The sun sinks into darkness each evening and is reborn at dawn, 'younger than the day before'. At each hour of the night a star is born, and at every instant there is a new birth. It would be difficult to express better the notion of a constant Becoming: each human being writes his name, the name that is his for a lifetime, in one of the knotted loops on the infinite thread of Eternity.

Alexandre Piankoff, one of the foremost specialists in the study of Egyptian myths, particularly those inscribed in the royal tombs, observed in 1953 that here, 'as with most of the great philosophical conceptions of the ancient world, the key is lost and we are too often tempted to apply the vague term of "mysticism". This is not mystical but physical science, as the Egyptians of the New Kingdom understood it'.

Let us re-envisage, in this spirit, the adventures of the twins, Shu and Tefnut, pursued and brought back three times by the Creator's enraged Eye. In the hieroglyphic writing, three marks depict not only the number three but also the plural form. Thus it may be that the twins take not just three but many journeys. As Shu represents Space, we are quite probably dealing with a representation of extreme dilation, followed by a contraction produced by the 'flame of the Eye', this alternation occurring a number of times and enduring for 'aeonic' periods. Now this 'cosmic pulsation' incites us to cast a curious glance at our modern conceptions of the origin and dynamics of the Universe.

Since modern technological means of investigation have enabled the immensities of the cosmos to be sounded, it has been observed that an enormous quantity of galaxies people the Universe. By virtue of the 'red shift' in the spectral study of the galaxies, Edwin Hubble and Milton Humason discovered that these galaxies ceaselessly move away from each other with an ever increasing speed, a phenomenon which gave rise to the hypothesis that the Universe is expanding. As a corollary to this, the 'Big Bang' hypothesis emerged, according to which there was a colossal explosion of an original atom in which all the potentialities of the Universe were concentrated – a supposition which in turn poses the problem of how it all ends.

In 1978 a group of scientists from Princeton University directed by J.Peebles pointed out that if the galaxies are very massive their gravitational attraction will ultimately halt the expansion, and the Universe will then enter into a phase of contraction. If, on the contrary, the galaxies are lighter than a certain critical mass, the present expansion of the Universe must continue indefinitely. Apparently the problem remains unsolved.

Already in 1956, in *Frontiers of Astronomy*, Fred Hoyle was seeking an explanation for the expansion of the universe which would eliminate the necessity of an initial explosion. It is wrong, he said, to assume that the observed expansion necessarily implies a single, superdense, then explosive origin of the Universe: this hypothesis is not valid unless all the matter existing today existed in the past. Among his suggestions was an inversion of Newton's theory of gravitation, to the effect that in the case of weak densities there would be a repulsion instead of the normal attraction.

Hoyle has now put forth some proposals: given that everything in the universe seems to undergo cyclic change, one might postulate, for example, that the mass of an electron might increase over a long period of time. In this case the size of its orbits (the atom's total diameter) would necessarily diminish. This possibility would call in question the Big Bang and the expanding universe hypothesis.

He suggests that the laws of the conservation of matter and energy observed in laboratories, as well as the laws of thermodynamics and entropy on which 'Big Bang' cosmological theory is based, are perhaps not immutable and might even not be applicable to cosmology at all. Instead of seeing the Universe as constantly threatened with collapse because of the laws of entropy, Hoyle proposes anew the idea that matter is in a state of constant creation. The Universe, he says, is infinite: it had no beginning and will have no end. Every cluster of galaxies, every star, every atom had a beginning, but not the Universe itself; the Universe is thus something more than its parts.

This conclusion brings us back to our ancient text, 'All that has been created will return into the Nun ... Myself alone, I persist.' 'I', that from which absolutely everything comes forth. This is the mystery of every instant, retold at each initiatory centre.

There is then on one hand, the eternal, and on the other, cyclic life. In myth, the eternal or immanent is called Atum, Amun, Rê or Ptah, according to which phase of genesis is being expressed; and the principle of the perpetual return of cyclic life is called Osiris.

The periodic return of the seasons and lunations, on which the symbolism of Osiris principally rests, governs all vegetation, and is the essential content of the celebrated Festivals of the Month of Khoiak, called by the classical authors the 'Mysteries'.

Already in the Pyramid Texts, Osiris was likened either to Orion – whose heliacal rising preceded that of Sirius, harbinger of the Nile's flood – or to the Moon.

> You are born in your months like the moon,
> Rê supports himself on you at the horizon.
> (Pyramid Texts, 732.)
> You appear at the new moon.
> (Pyramid Texts, 1012.)

The lunar month begins on the day of the new moon, as is specified here by the allusion to the conjunction of Rê and Osiris (sun and moon), found together on the horizon.

Another passage from these same texts deals with the harvesting of spelt (a primitive form of wheat) and the threshing of barley – the end of a cycle of vegetation – and the offering of grain to Osiris, promising him perpetuity through resurrection. These ceremonies are described and depicted in six small chambers divided into two groups, one on the north-west and the other on the south-east end of the roof-terrace of the Temple of Hathor at Dendera. In the first of these is found the procession of priests from Upper and Lower Egypt, each carrying the emblem of his province.

Long hymns celebrate the presence of Osiris in each part of the country, and at the same time it is precisely specified which are the fourteen (or sixteen) sanctuaries in which the sacred relics were deposited.

The two central chambers are consecrated to cosmic entities who contribute to the establishment of an atmosphere favourable to the realization of the mystery of the resurrection. This mystery was reserved for the deepest and darkest sanctuaries.

In the middle room of the north-west group the walls are occupied by the entities of the decans, days and hours, and by the guardians of the twelve gates through which the sun must pass during the day. This is very important and enables us to glimpse a solution to the as yet unexplained scene on the ceiling. Nut, the Sky, who is shown arched over in her usual manner, has solar discs instead of the conventional stars on her belly, suggesting that it is the sun's diurnal course that is being described. Nut swallows the sun in the evening and gives birth to it again in the morning; and so the sun's *daytime* path starts from her pubis and goes to her mouth.

On the ground, Geb, the Earth, attracts our attention by his strange position, suggesting a somersault; in other words, a revolution on himself. This takes place in the inverse direction to the apparent course of the sun. It is difficult to avoid seeing an allusion here to the rotation of the earth on itself, in the direction opposite to that of the apparent movement of the sky. (Note that the position of the tableau when placed on the ceiling will be the inverse of what it is when before us on the paper.) Furthermore, knowing that the height of man is very nearly equal to his armspan, Geb's extended arms measure the length of the circuit that his body will make.

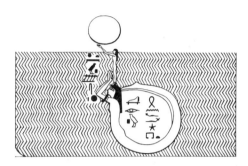

This image, of Osiris encircling the Dwat or 'inverted world' carrying on his head Nut (the Sky), who receives the sun, also evokes a circuit or daily revolution. Note that the rotational movement of Osiris is counter-clockwise, the direction of our earth's spin.

On the ceiling in the parallel room of the south-east group, next to a large axial female figure of the sky with elongated arms, Nut is found in her arched position, enframing fourteen small barques (a lunar number), and on the other side is the famous circular zodiac (a cast of the original now in the Louvre in Paris). The centre of the zodiac medallion is occupied by the cluster of circumpolar stars. On an off-set circle following the ecliptic are situated the twelve zodiacal constellations. Around the outside are

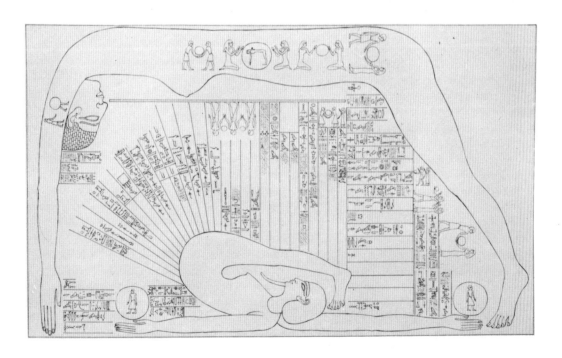

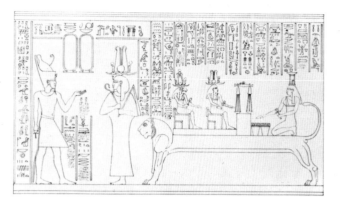

several southern constellations, among which are Sirius and Orion, and finally, on the periphery, are found the thirty-six decans of the complete annual cycle (see pp. 74–5).

Protective birds and entities armed with swords line the walls of this chamber, along with the divinities of the twenty-four hours of the day and night, guarding against disturbance and so maintaining the best conditions for carrying out the reawakening of Osiris.

In each of the temples containing Osiris' sacred relics, a 'seed bed' had to be made every year as an effigy of Osiris, and filled with soil. A golden image of Osiris was deposited in it, along with the sacred relic. The seed bed was then sown with grains of spelt and carefully watered.

Simultaneously, a statuette of Sokar (a protohistoric falcon-headed divinity, assimilated to Osiris) was fashioned with twenty-four metals and the aromatics preserved in the 'divine vase'. Fourteen amulets of precious stones were placed on the fourteen related body parts, and finally 104 other amulets of various kinds were added to them.

These two symbols were the object of constant ceremonies, in the course of which, for example, two pieces of cloth were woven. On the tenth day a great procession took place. The retinue crossed the desert, preceded by four obelisks whose pyramidions were ornamented with images of four genii. Then the night festival took place, illuminated by 365 lamps, while thirty-four small papyrus barques containing statuettes of the local Ennead and corresponding entities floated on the sacred lake.

On each side of the door giving access to the deepest sanctuary at Dendera is found a tableau in which Isis on one side and Nepthys on the other are called Shen-tyt, a name meaning 'they who preside over the cycles' – in other words, over the periodic revolutions of nature.

The two divinities, seated on beds in front of the vases in which the grains will germinate, and the scales thought to balance the elementary and cosmic powers, are seen to proclaim that they 'render the plants fertile, make them grow by their action, and give the wheat its sprouting power, without cease'.

Seated on two thrones on the other side of the scales are Ptah, the blacksmith Creator of Memphis (at the apex of the Delta), and Khnum of Elephantine (on the southern border), the divine potter, modeller of men and things. These two contribute to the germination of the grain, and claim, in the inscription, to protect the growth of the wheat in the dwelling of the two Shen-tyt.

The germination of the grain therefore appears to be the essential theme of the Festivals of Khoiak, as described in the Temple of Dendera, and published by Auguste Mariette Pasha, who wrote of them:

The grain of wheat, appearing inert when planted in the ground, is Osiris in the tomb; the grain which germinates, and produces the head of wheat from which will come the bread and nourishment of man, is the god who, under the sweet influence of the two Shen-tyt, comes to life again in order to heap his favours on earth. . . . Everything in nature lives to die, and dies in order to be reborn.

Mariette concludes with the phrase from the *Pymander* of Hermes Trismegistus, 'There where everything ends, all begins eternally.'

Of the two figures of Osiris standing before the royal figure, the one with Nepthys (on the left) is the representative of the city of Busiris, and the one with Isis (on the right) represents Abydos.

In the deepest sanctuary our attention is drawn first of all by two series of seven barques. The first is that of Sokar, the divinity identified with Osiris, cited in the Pyramid Texts as a metal-founder. This relates him to Ptah, the divine blacksmith of Memphis, making up the strange triad of Ptah-Sokar-Osiris venerated there.

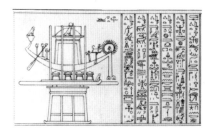

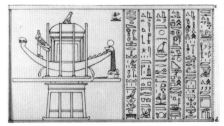

Next come two barques whose bows are decorated with shining discs, clearly indicating their relation with the solar circuit. The fourth, called the 'barque of the new moon', is characterized by a tiny pig at its stern – this being the animal which is said to 'eat the moon'. The three other barques are in relation with the four cardinal directions. Each is accompanied by a hymn exhorting Osiris to raise himself up triumphantly out of obstacles, death and darkness, and reappear each hour like the stars, each day like the radiant sun, each month like the moon, each year like Orion, his youth restored each time, in perpetuity.

At ground level, pictured in a golden barque, is Osiris 'who has taken his place in the sun', and is thus triumphant. He is assimilated to Horus of the Double Horizon (the solar globe) as well as to the serpent Sa-ta, who is raised up before him as the symbol of the arable land enriched by the flood. The adjacent scene shows Osiris lying on the ritual lion-headed bed, inhaling the perfume of the lotus held for him by the Child Horus who, by his own growth, 'makes the vegetation become'.

front of 'Horus son of Isis who protects his father'. At Bubastis, the divine soul perched on a tree protects the golden image with eyes of lapis lazuli, awaiting the moment to reincarnate in it. At Busiris, 'Osiris is he who exists from the beginning. All is within him, he is the master of perpetuity, he rises at dawn and sets at night like the sun, eternally'.

At Abydos, Sokar-Osiris, Master of the Mysteries of the Resurrection, is figured in the course of the different phases of his reawakening to life.

On the last day of the month of Khoiak the burial of the seed-bed and the statues of the year takes place. They are interred in a mound of earth shaded with persea trees.

This same day, the resurrection of Osiris is publicly celebrated by the erection of the Djed pillar or Osirian column – a beautiful representation of which can be seen in the Temple of Abydos. This ceremony was public and according to all the known calendars took place on the 30th of Khoiak (mid-November, if we follow the 'vague year' or 25 December in the Alexandrian calendar).

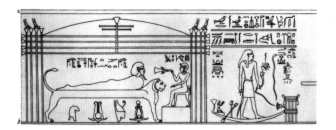

Finally come the twenty-nine beds (as many as there are days in a lunation), divided between the two chapels, upon which rest the local Osirises, each taking the position and attributes particular to one of the cities rendering him worship. Thus, at Hermopolis in the north, Osiris is raised up on his right side (whereas he had fallen on his left) in

Return

Initiation
At Sais is found the tomb of Him whom I hesitate to name. . . . On the lake (of the temple) at night, the Egyptians give a representation of the suffering undergone by Him: they call them the Mysteries. . . . About these Mysteries, all of which, without exception, are known to me, may my lips maintain a religious silence. (Herodotus.)

Of the things which are enacted as worship, some have a mysterious significance and are impossible to render in words; others represent [allegorically] some other image, just as Nature expresses the visible forms of hidden reasons. (Iamblichus.)

It is the perfect execution, transcending the intelligence, of ineffable acts; it is the inexplicable force of symbols, which gives us awareness of divine things. (Iamblichus.)

In the *Metamorphoses* of Apuleius – *The Golden Ass* – the neophyte Lucius, after having followed an ascetic regime for ten days, is led into the deepest sanctuary where he passes the night. He then says,

I have no doubt, curious reader, that you are eager to know what happened when I entered. If I were allowed to tell you, and you were allowed to be told, you would soon hear everything; but as it is my tongue would suffer for its indiscretion and your ears for their inquisitiveness.

However, not wishing to leave you, if you are religiously inclined, in a state of tortured suspense, I will record as much as I may lawfully record for the uninitiated, but only on the condition that you believe it. I approached the very gates of death and set one foot on Proserpine's threshold, yet was permitted to return, rapt, through all the elements. At midnight I saw the sun shining as if it were noon; I entered the presence of the gods of the underworld and the gods of the upper world, stood near and worshipped them.

Well, now you have heard what happened, but I fear you are still none the wiser. (Trans. Robert Graves, p. 286.)

We can only conclude that, as Iamblichus counsels, the seeker must find the 'mysterious meaning' and the 'awareness of divine things' through ritual and symbols alone.

For example, from earliest antiquity a constant theme has been the dismemberment of Osiris. His members must then be brought back together, his bones purified and reassembled, etc. Now, instead of conventionally interpreting these acts as vestiges of a cannibalistic cult, or of the ritual murder of the king, might we not consider the striking parallelism between these texts and those of various ecstatic or initiatic visions, such as experienced by the Yakut shamans?

The Yakuts say that the future shaman 'dies and lies in the yurt [tent] for three days without eating or drinking', writes Mircea Eliade in *Shamanism*. It is said that 'formerly the candidate went through the ceremony three times, during which he was cut to pieces. The candidate's members are removed and disjointed with an iron hook, the bones are cleaned, the flesh scraped, the body liquids thrown away and the eyes torn out from their sockets.' We find in the Pyramid Texts:

[King] Wnas was liberated from the humanity which is in his members ... Horus has received him between his fingers, he purifies him in the lake of the jackal, he brushes the flesh of the royal double. (Pyramid Texts, 371–373.)

Oh arise! You have received your head, your bones are reassembled, your members are rejoined to you. Shake off the dust! (Pyramid Texts, 654.)

And the King is given back the use of his eyes and mouth with a hook of meteoric iron. (Pyramid Texts, 13–14.)

Another of Eliade's sources recounts that the shamans receive the power of healing through a bird of prey with an iron beak and hooked claws, which 'cuts the body of the candidate into bits and distributes them among the evil spirits of disease and death.' After they have devoured the entire body, these spirits leave; then the mythic birds put the bones back in place and the future shaman awakens, endowed with the power to cure the maladies in question. Many are the tales and cultural contexts in which the basic theme of dismemberment, apparent death, reconstitution and resurrection recurs.

Among the Iglulik Eskimos a sequence of initiations concludes with the *angakoq*, meaning 'lightening' or 'illumination'. This *angakoq* consists of 'a mysterious light which the shaman suddenly feels in his body, inside his head, within his brain, an inexplicable searchlight, a luminous fire which enables him to see with both eyes, both literally and metaphorically speaking, for he can now, even with closed eyes, see through darkness and perceive things and coming events which are hidden from others'.

It is impossible not to relate this inner light to the Pharaonic word for light, *akh*. This word, often translated as 'transfigured', designates transcendental light as well as all aspects of physical light; and in the funerary texts it denotes the state of ultimate sublimation.

The subtle elements of the being
According to the funerary texts, man is composed of a mortal body, *kha*, and principally of three subtle, immortal elements, *akh*, *ba* and *ka*. These were formerly translated respectively as 'spirit', 'soul' and 'double', but these words are much too limited to express the concepts implied.

The word *akh*, first of all, is written with a glyph showing a crested ibis, *Ibis comata*. This bird – the name of which was also *akh* – lived in the southern part of the Arabian side of the Red Sea (near Al Qunfidhah) and migrated to Abyssinia during winter. Both these places are near the regions from which sacred incense came, and were called the 'Divine Land'. The bird's crest, together with its dark

green plumage shot with glittering metallic specks, justifies the meanings 'to shine', 'to be resplendent', 'to irradiate', of the root *akh* in the hieroglyphic writing.

Akh indeed expresses all notions of light, both literally and figuratively, from the Light which comes forth from Darkness to the transcendental light of transfiguration. It is also used to designate the 'third eye', the *uraeus*, related in the old tradition to the pineal body and to the spirit.

In the cosmogonic myths, *akh* appears as the aspect of spirit which conceives in advance what the object of the creation will be, a notion comparable to Plato's Ideas.

Akh pre-exists the Creation, and it is also its final goal. When, in a funerary text, the king is addressed in the other world with the words 'You are more *akh* than the *akhw*', we should understand that pure spirit, after it has descended and incarnated in matter in order to become conscious in that condition, returns to the 'pre-existent *akhw*' enriched, with knowledge of itself and of all manifestation. Light is thus transfigured. Thus it is written that 'the king returns to the right hand of his father' (Pyramid Texts, 267–268).

It is certainly evident that spirit, *akh*, as the opposite of the perishable body, *kha*, is immortal. '*Akh* is for heaven, *kha* is for earth', we read in the Pyramid Texts.

All this serves to make more comprehensible the names, at first sight startling, of the seven souls (*baw*) of the Supreme Being, Rê: Soul of the Pure Seed; Soul of the Unscathed Flesh; Glorious and Blossoming Soul; Magic-soul; Essence-soul; Male soul; Soul that Copulates.

The *ba* incarnates itself; it defines the character and affinities of the individual, 'each according to its nature'.

The word *ba* has several aspects:

– expressed in the plural, *baw*, it is the cosmic soul, the breath of life in all of nature;

– symbolized by the ram with horizontal horns, it is the soul animating all those beings who, like Osiris, are subject to cyclic rebirth;

– represented by the human-headed bird, it symbolizes the human soul.

Two ways are offered to our soul after death: either a final liberation or a return into incarnation in order to continue the experience of becoming conscious. Many are the texts alluding to reincarnation, either overtly or implicitly through such locutions as 'renewal of life' or 'repetition of births'. (This eventuality explains the choice of a migratory bird to designate the *ba*.)

The Judgment of the Dead takes place in the 'Hall of the Double Maât'. This judgment is made in the presence of

The mortal body *kha* is animated during its existence by the *ba*, written with a migratory bird, the jabiru or stork, accompanied by a pot with a flame burning in it, or else represented in the form of a human-headed bird fluttering about the tomb near the dead person.

The *ba* also plays a role in cosmogenesis. We have seen, for example, that the soul, *ba*, of Shu was the fire produced by Atum at the moment of the initial creative emission of semen. Likewise the Creator 'made metamorphoses starting from this, his *ba*', the *ba* thus playing the role of the determining individualizing force, the first active principle, parallel to the first coagulation, the disruption of the inertia in the cosmic ocean.

the dead person's consciousness, Maât, while the other Maât, cosmic consciousness, presides at the weighing of his heart. Placed on one of the pans of the scale, and weighed against the feather of Maât, the heart expresses the feelings and passions which, if too heavy, risk drawing the soul back again towards earth.

The *ka* is a complex idea for which we have no linguistic counterpart at all. It is currently thought that the *ka* is a manifestation of vital energy, but this fails to explain why statues, formulas and offerings are dedicated, in the funerary ritual, to the *ka*; or why a narrow 'false door' is left in the tomb for the *ka* to come and go and eat of the food figured on the walls.

The *ka*, an abstract principle, was formerly translated as 'double', for it seemed inherent in every living thing. In the Room of the Theogamy at Luxor, for example, we find on the lower register, Khnum, the ram-headed divine potter from the first cataract, as the modeller of both the divine child and his *ka*. In the middle register, depicting the child's birth, the infant *ka*, recognizable by the symbol of the two upraised arms that he wears on his head, awaits the birth of his twin. Two of the divine midwives then present both infants to Amun. Finally on the upper register the two children are being suckled by the divinities, then by the celestial cows, before being presented by personifications of magic power (Heka) and the Nile (Hapy), who give them both life and prosperity. The infants are preceded by Horus, and it is written that all the purifications are made in 'this place of the birth of Horus-Seth'. This phrase is of the greatest importance, for it reveals that the *ka* can be considered as the inverse of the being in the same way that Seth is of Horus. In this case the *ka* or 'double' is indissociable from the physically existing individual. A schist cup, dating from the Thinite period (First Dynasty) bears two linked hieroglyphic signs, *ka* and *ankh*, which must signify '*ka* gives life' (see p. 71).

In an important chapter of the Book of the Dead the deceased identifies himself with Osiris and declares that he knows 'the rebirths of Rê [the sun] and his metamorphoses which take place in the flood [the Nun]'. He adds that he knows not only the names of the seven souls (*baw*) but also those of the fourteen *kaw*, which the context shows to be related to rebirth, through reincarnation.

For example, on the lower register of the north wall of the burial chamber in the tomb of Ramses VI, the solar barque is drawn by seven *baw* before foundering in the waters of the Nun, from which the solar globe re-emerges, regenerated, drawn by the fourteen *kaw*.

These fourteen *kaw* can be grouped in pairs and symbolize the maintenance of life:

ka subsistence	*ka* nutrition
ka of *kaw* (creative power of food)	*ka* greenness (that which develops, causes to thrive)
ka penetration	*ka* consideration
ka venerability	*ka* vassalage (the honour of serving a respected master)
ka force	*ka* worth
ka splendour	*ka* radiance
ka magic	*ka* illumination

These fourteen epithets are revelatory of the fundamental qualities attached to the notion of the *ka*. The first four are self-explanatory, evidently being the vitalizing powers of food, enabling the development, growth and subsistence of all of physical life. Yet prior to everything, appetite or attraction is needed, symbolized by the two upraised arms in a gesture of calling, the hieroglyph of *ka*.

The following epithets express the moral qualities and social condition of the being. These imply submission to a discipline, but also an appetite or thirst for perfection which can act as a stimulus, giving an immediate goal to human life.

The last two, magic (mastery) and illumination, probably represent the ultimate spiritual call of the being, realizable only through the force and worth of each person's character, giving him splendour and radiance while still in life.

The *ka* thus appears as the abstract element symbolizing an individual's 'tendencies', or physical, moral and spiritual 'appetites', which are likely, if they remain unsatisfied, to attract the soul *ba* towards a new incarnation.

With the reservation, then, that the words only approach the true meanings, we can say that spirit, *akh*, incarnates in the body, *kha*, which the soul *ba* animates during its life and escapes at death. The *ka* remains more or less attached to terrestrial life and eventually recalls the being to be born again – if necessary.

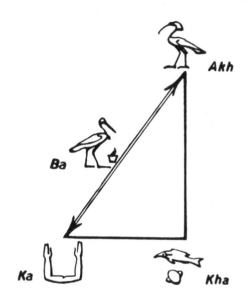

Funerary rituals
The Egyptians' particular conception of the human complex, and especially that of the *ka*, incites one to search for these notions in the earliest historical sources available to us.

The most ancient burial grounds known date from the Neolithic period, although it should be remembered that the Nile, after having hollowed out its bed, built up its embankments by annually depositing silt in such a way that it is not impossible that one or several previous civilizations were buried.

In the Neolithic period the dead were deposited in oval graves in foetal position, with the head at the south. In Lower Egypt the deceased was placed on his right side, his face turned towards the east, while in Upper Egypt, as all along the upper Nile, the dead person was placed on his left side, looking west. Often the body was wrapped in a cloth or an animal skin, the head resting on a cushion.

The tomb contained objects used by the individual in life, and in many cases the hand nearest the mouth had been strewn with grains of wheat. The presence of these grains reveals the idea of making food offerings to the dead; perhaps this is the prototype of this same custom, addressed to the *ka* during the entire historic period. As for the foetal position, the interpretation which seems most obvious is that of rebirth through reincarnation – as, for example, in a descendant – after a long sleep at the breast of the Earth Mother: a belief found at many points of the globe.

In Dynastic Egypt, the papyri now designated by the name of 'Book of the Dead' because they were discovered placed on the bodies of dead individuals, are actually entitled 'Book of the Coming Forth into Day, to Live after Death'. These 'books' are composed of nearly two hundred formulae that it was believed the deceased ought to know in order to be able to escape the snares which could interfere with his ascension to Heaven. The title of the famous Chapter 17 summarizes the programme of the whole:

Beginning of the elevations, glorifications of the going out, of the descent into the burial ground. To come forth into day, to make all the metamorphoses that one desires ... to come forth as a living soul, after death.

It is evidently the living soul which must be able to 'come and go at its pleasure'; but although the idea of rebirth is persistently implied, it is formally affirmed only in two popular tales. In the Tale of Satni, a magician-sage reincarnates in the form of a child whose parents conceived him after having eaten a certain plant, in a particular place which was indicated to them in a dream. In the famous Tale of Two Brothers, the protagonist Bata, 'soul of bread', has been compared with Osiris since both were emasculated and their virile members thrown into the Nile. Bata's was swallowed by the catfish, *nar*, and that of Osiris by *khat*, the fish *Oxyrhynchus* or *Mormyrus*, the hieroglyph of which designates the cadaver and in general, everything putrifiable.

Bata, victim of a woman's waywardness and betrayal, died for the first time when a tree was felled whose top held the flower of his 'heart' or vital principle. Bata returned to life after the seed of this flower had been recovered and moistened. But, transformed into a bull, he was again killed and two drops of blood fell on the ground, giving birth to two magnificent persea trees. These were also chopped

down, but a chip of wood jumped into the mouth of the woman who had first betrayed him; she immediately became pregnant and gave birth once more to Bata. Here the tale evokes the miraculous birth of Horus, born of the posthumous union of Isis and Osiris.

These instances of rebirth through the vegetable kingdom recall the 'Mysteries of Osiris' described at Dendera, which are completed only by a piece of information found in the Jumiliac Papyrus. Here a vase containing the humours of Osiris, coveted by Seth, is stolen several times, then recaptured by Thoth, then by Anubis, Horus and Isis and kept in a holy place. Of this place it is written,

... these are the divine humours which have sprouted into fruit trees.
... the Double Land is inundated thanks to the divine humours, causing divinities and men to live.
... this is the temple in which [the mummies] live, finding once more a vegetable life in the form of wheat and spelt.

Royal Tombs: The Two Ways
At Abydos in the Thinite nome or province, the place where Osiris was particularly venerated, a large necropolis was discovered at the end of the last century, in close proximity to arable land. Only the infrastructures of the tombs remained intact. These consisted of a chamber for the sarcophagus and numerous storerooms in which inscribed objects were found, enabling the tombs to be dated. For example, the famous stela of the Serpent King, belonging to King Djt, the third monarch of the First Dynasty, was among them. Since, according to Manetho, these kings bore the epithet of 'Thinite', it was logical to think that they had been buried here in their own province.

It was therefore with some amazement that, approximately half a century later, archaeologists discovered about fifteen edifices on the plateau near ancient Memphis, north of Saqqara. These were of unfired brick, in very large dimensions, and characterized by façades in modulated planes, with recessed panels. The many objects found in their storerooms enabled them to be attributed, without hesitation, to the very same kings as the hypogea at Abydos. Now, even supposing that the larger northern mastabas of Memphis were the true burials, and that those in the south were only cenotaphs, the question remains: why in the First Dynasty did the kings apparently have two tombs?

The funerary edifices of King Zoser of the Third Dynasty raised the same problem. Zoser's complex, including the step-pyramid and the courts of his Sed Festival (or Jubilee), is bounded by a magnificent wall, which encloses an area 550 metres (a third of a mile) long and about half that in width. This wall is an imitation in limestone of the recessed, stepped façades of the unfired brick mastabas of the First Dynasty. Likewise, in the interior, the stone covers of the apartments imitate the wooden mouldings of the ancient ceilings, and numerous other architectural details serve to fix in stone the outlines of the earlier brick buildings.

Thus, when it was further observed that there were two tombs in the compound, one in the northern part, under the pyramid, and the other at the south, near the enclosing wall, there was every reason to believe that the complex demonstrated the maintenance of an older tradition.

The northern funerary vault, made of granite, probably replaces a similar one of fine limestone, the cover of which was decorated with stars on both the outside and inside faces. Its dimensions conform to the proportions of a normal sarcophagus, which, if similar to those of the royal children found under the pyramid, was probably of laminated wood, plated with gold.

The vault in the south resembled the northern one except that it was square and much too small to have contained a human body. The initial puzzlement as to its function was resolved by excavations demonstrating that other, much later kings had two coffins, one containing the mummy and the other the four canopic vases holding the internal organs. This custom, which endured throughout the historic period, was thus revealed to be very ancient.

It was then necessary to acknowledge that the First Dynasty kings had two burial places, and that these were far apart: one for the canopic vases at the southern city of Abydos and the other for the mummy near Memphis in the north – cities more than 560 kilometres (350 miles) apart. This was an astonishing fact, and stimulated investigation into the possible reasons behind it.

Let us recall that at the time of the presentation of the royal infant and his *ka* or double to Amun, mention was made, in the accompanying text, of Horus and Seth.

Corresponding to Horus, Master of the North, is the dilation of the heart, the spiritual quest for transcendent light symbolized by the search for the 'Eye'. It is therefore in the north that the mummy, the receptacle of the divine spark during existence, now freed from decomposition, was respectfully buried.

Corresponding to Seth, Lord of the South, are the contractive functions assimilated to those of semen (the testicles are his symbol): those of physical, terrestrial continuity. Thus in the south the *ka* can exercise to the maximum its capacity of 'calling' and manifest its appetite, the reason that it was symbolically offered food items. The south then was the burial place for the vital organs, the animal parts of man.

But here a macrocosmic interpretation asserts itself. The Pyramid Texts abound with statements concerning the so-called 'stellar destiny' of the King. The King's soul is thrust into heaven to become a star, or else it ascends by means of a ladder constructed, held together and supported by divine entities. The King then takes his place in the retinue of Rê or presides over the circumpolar stars:

The sky thunders, the earth quakes, Geb shudders, the two regions roar . . . when [the King] rises up to heaven, traverses the firmament [*bia*], crosses Lake Hsaw, destroying the ramparts of Shu [space]. He ascends to the sky; the tips of his wings are like those of a great bird. His entrails have been washed by Anubis while the encircling of Horus and the embalming of Osiris have been carried out at Abydos.

He climbs to the sky among the Imperishable Stars. (Pyramid Texts, 1120–23.)

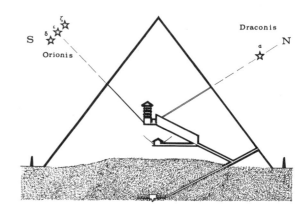

Egypt, it was said, is in the image of Heaven. The emphasis placed on north and south then leads us to investigate the regions of the sky, of which earth is only a reflection.

A north/south section of the Pyramid of Cheops shows that the two so-called 'air-shafts' leading out from the King's Chamber are, within one degree of accuracy, inclined so that the northern one is centred on the celestial Pole and the southern one on the three stars of Orion's Belt. In her presentation of these facts, Virginia Trimble pointed out that, in the light of the ancients' mystic sense, it is obvious that these openings were meant to be guide-ways for the soul, aiming either towards the Circumpolars in the northern sky or to the constellation of Orion in the southern sky.

It is actually a matter of two ways being offered to each individual: that of final liberation and eternal life (the north), or that of reincarnation in a mortal body and the commencement of a new experience (the south).

In the north at the approximate time of the pyramid's construction in 2700 BC, the Pole was occupied by Alpha Draconis, the star around which turned the Circumpolars – called the 'Indestructibles' since they never disappear below the horizon. Thus they were the symbol of immortality. The King then, triumphant over the trials of terrestrial life, will ascend imperishable in the northern sky.

From the southern sky, the ancients had chosen thirty-six stars or constellations, the decans, whose consecutive heliacal risings occurred approximately every ten days. The rising of each decan occurred after it had passed seventy days of invisibility, a period corresponding to that of mummification. Among these stars are Osiris (Orion) and Isis-Sothis (Sirius), symbols of yearly renewal, of the regeneration of the Nile, of cyclic death and rebirth.

From the earliest examples, whenever the inner sides of coffin lids or tomb ceilings were decorated, allusion was made to the starry sky. In the Middle Kingdom coffin lids were divided longitudinally into twelve lines corresponding to the twelve hours of the night and into thirty-six vertical divisions on which the circuit of the decans in the course of the year was inscribed. The dedicatory band divided this 'sky' into two parts. On one side Nut raises her arms to aid the deceased in his ascent. She stands next to 'the Thigh which is in the northern sky' – that is the Great Bear, recognizable by its seven stars. On the other side is Orion, who 'is in the southern sky', his face turned backwards, and Sirius or Sothis, who 'gives life'.

In the New Kingdom the royal tombs are grouped on the Nile's western bank at Thebes, in the famous Valley of the Kings, dominated by a pyramid-shaped mountain called 'The Peak' in ancient times. In the Eighteenth Dynasty (about 1600–1300 BC), at the end of zigzagging tomb galleries hollowed out of the cliffs, are found vaults whose walls are covered with an immense unrolled painted papyrus. This is the 'Book of What is in the Dwat', which is found in identical form in the royal tombs of the following dynasties as well.

In the Nineteenth Dynasty (about 1300 BC), the rectilinear galleries, attaining a length of sometimes more than a hundred metres, are entirely covered with 'Books'. On the ceilings, Nut is depicted with arched body, swallowing the sun in the evening and giving birth to it again in the morning. Her star- and globe-strewn body indicates the twelve hours of the night and the twelve hours of the day. All the decans and constellations of both the northern and southern skies are enumerated in great detail (see pp. 74–75).

Written on the walls of these tombs, in addition to the Book of What is in the Dwat, are:

– the Book of Caverns, describing mysterious dens harbouring numerous serpents and the shadowy depths in which the gestation of the new sun is brought about;

– the Book of Gates, so designated because twelve gates guarded by terrifying fire-spitting serpents mark the twelve divisions which the solar barque must cross during its nocturnal course;

– the Book of Aker, composed of a group of particularly enigmatic tableaux, and represented nearly uniquely in the tomb of Ramses VI.

The Book of What is in the Dwat

'The writings in the secret chamber', that is the royal sarcophagus room, concern the journey of the 'Great Neter' in his barque through the Dwat, the realm of the twelve hours of the night. Each hour has a name, a guide, a gate and a particular guardian.

The divine boat navigates on a central river on whose banks numerous entities enact roles which vary according to the character of each hour. Often protective entities, they define the environment and can be related to celestial or terrestrial phenomena. All of them, however, came forth from the members of the Supreme Being, here called Rê.

When this divine principle animates the solar globe he is called Khepri in the morning, Rê at noon, and Atum in the evening. In the Dwat he bears still another name, Iwf, which we will return to shortly.

The principal figure in the divine boat has a ram's head, with horns surmounted by a disc. Sceptre in hand, he stands within a *naos* or tabernacle during the first six hours, the descent, and within the coils of the spiral serpent Mehen for the last six hours, the re-ascent.

At the front of the boat is the 'Opener of the Ways', followed by Sia, 'Knowledge', and then the 'Mistress of the Barque'. Of the five figures in the back of the boat we should take note of Hw, 'The Word', standing just in front of the pilot.

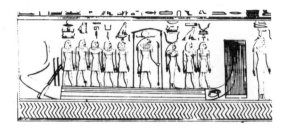

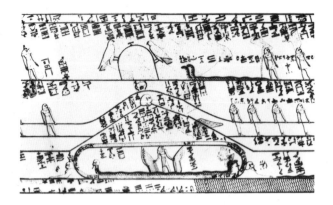

The central figure represents 'the soul of Rê', and his name, Iwf, 'Flesh', is curious indeed. However, the particular sense that this name is to be given here is defined with the insistence of several repetitions in the texts of the second and third hours:

'I have come here to see my body in order to inspect my image which is in the Dwat', says the Great Neter.

The divine entities answer, 'Come then to us, thou whose flesh sails, who is led towards his own body. . . . The sky is for thy soul, the earth for thy body. . . . Illumine the primordial darkness so that the "flesh" may live and renew itself. . . . [Thou art] He who becomes, He who metamorphoses himself toward the east.'

There is no doubt that we are dealing here with the incarnation – the becoming flesh – of the divine principle of light. This principle 'travels through the hours and lives in the barque of Khepri', say the texts in the first tableau, where indeed we find, under the solar barque, a skiff in which rides Khepri, the scarab, the future rising sun, framed by two Osirises symbolizing cyclic rebirths.

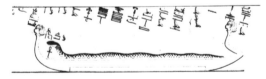

The Dwat is then the world of metamorphoses, of which the scarab Khepri is the pre-eminent symbol. He is found again on one of the barques in the second tableau where the divine entities must make darkness descend – as conducive to the germination of grains as it is to the development of the scarab's egg, enveloped in its dungball. Out of this dungball a worm or larva is born, symbolized by a serpent, sailing in the fourth hour on 'the secret ways taken by the cadaver of Sokar [Osiris]'.

We find this same serpent or larva again in the fifth hour in an ovoid cavern at the heart of the earth. This image plunged 'into the primordial darkness' represents 'the flesh and body of the first phenomenal form'. Rising out of the serpent's convolutions is the hawk-headed figure of Sokar, holding the wings which will be formed in the nymphalid phase in his hands. The 'mound of Sokar', protected from above by two birds (Isis and Nepthys), envelops the whole scene, concealing the mysteries . . . and nothing can reach them, for the paths leading into the mound are filled with flames.

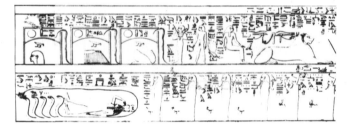

In the sixth hour the divine barque is steered by 'The one who hides his images', toward the 'many-headed serpent who bites his own tail' encircling the 'body of Khepri' (the man-scarab). The barque is preceded by a series of royal mummies. Above, three chests guarded by fire-spitting serpents contain a human head, a wing and the hindquarters of an animal, suggesting – as the philosophers of our Middle Ages would say – 'that there can be no metamorphosis without the destruction of the first form'. This is a general law. Behind the chests, the 'divine eyes' above the lion, 'the male with voice of thunder', remind us that on one of its levels the theme of this book is the regeneration of the sun. Finally Taït, a divinity of weaving, suggests that the moment for the making of the cocoon is drawing near. This is exactly so, for according to J.H.Fabre, the four phases of insect gestation each last for about the same amount of time, so that here, the first three hours correspond to the gestation and incubation of the egg, then the fourth through the sixth to the nourishment of the larva, and the seventh through ninth hours to the metamorphosis into nymph. The nymph or pupa startlingly recalls the mummy enveloped in its wrappings.

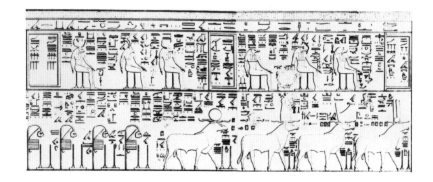

Indeed, in the eighth hour we find all the entities, except those hauling the barque, seated on strips of woven cloth. And at the end of the middle register are four rams which, the hieroglyphs say, represent the four metamorphoses.

In the tenth hour, the beginning of the final phase, the scarab pushes his oval 'cocoon', while the birth of the left and right Eyes, the moon and the sun, are announced. The left Eye emerges from between entwined serpents and the right Eye from the symbol for Neter, 'divinity'.

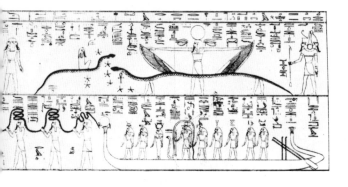

The eleventh hour shows a small human figure seated on a serpent, taking off for the stars, but the texts concerning this scene – as well as the neighbouring winged serpent – tell us nothing of its meaning. The two-headed figures alone seem to inform us that in this place the union of opposites is realized.

In the twelfth hour, 'His Majesty the Great Neter arrives at the cavern at the end of the primordial darkness where he will take birth under his phonomenal form as Khepri'. *Uraei* protect him and entities acclaim him from the riverbanks. 'The soul of the Master of Heaven, which is sublimated in him', is born and shall 'become'.

At the centre of the tableau, in his barque, 'This Neter thus sails in this his place, in the vertebral column of this secret image of the serpent 'Divine Life', while his Neterw haul him. . . . The Imakhw [blessed] of Rê who are behind and in front of him ... enter into the secret image of the serpent ... who lives from the murmur of the Imakhw who are in his marrow [*imakh*].'

The entire meaning of this extraordinary image rests on the word *imakh* which means both marrow and ultimate sublimation, the supreme beatitude of the being freed from all physical contingencies.

This represents the apotheosis of the evolution of the human being. The Book of What is in the Dwat can thus be summarized: The soul becomes incarnate in Flesh [Iwf]. In the course of time, it undergoes the vicissitudes of physical existence and the metabolic processes through which food breaks down and becomes flesh and blood, then nervous substance and finally marrow, the most subtle part of us, for it directs all our activity, from physical movement to thought, the impalpable, supreme abstraction.

Thus the passage of the Great Neter and his retinue through the serpent's marrow is a marvellous symbol of sublimation and spiritual liberation. The point could not be better expressed than by the abandoned mummy of flesh lying on the ground: the triumph of Light over Darkness.

Everything comes forth from the Nun, the primordial cosmic ocean, the eternal and infinite source. At the time of the inundation, which transforms the country into a veritable sea, Hapy, the Nile, re-enacts the mystery of the Origin. Then the floodwaters recede, recalling the appearance of the 'first earth' and the process of Creation. Each geographic region in Egypt expresses one of the phrases of this genesis or another aspect of the myth. Thus the entire topography of the country is recalled in the bas-reliefs carved on the bases of temples along the Nile. Pictured standing or kneeling, wearing the characteristic beard of his male aspect as the inseminator, but with a protruding belly and essentially nourishing breast, each 'Nile' wears a grid on his head representing the system of canals irrigating the terrain, and the characteristic emblems of his province. There were 38 to 42 provinces, some of which dated from prehistoric times. (Nile figure of the 15th Nome, Temple of Ramses II, Abydos, Nineteenth Dynasty, c. 1250 B C.)

The Nile is one of the longest rivers in the world and crosses the world's largest desert. Since the remotest antiquity it has been known for its exceptional rhythm. Each year during the Dog Days (around the time of the heliacal rising of Sirius, the Dog Star), it starts to enlarge and swell until, overrunning its banks, it floods the entire valley. For nearly three months the Nile covers all Egypt with its waters, causing her to resemble the Primordial Ocean, say the texts, and depositing the precious silt that fertilizes the earth.

Whereas absolutely nothing grows on the rocky desert cliffs, the hollow of the valley is a rich, verdant oasis, populated by numerous herds.

At Saqqara, in the tombs of the Old Kingdom, bearers of offerings, such as these from the Tomb of Ty, symbolize the towns and domains which were under the rulership of the Nomarch. They carry baskets on their heads exactly as do the country people of today, or like the women who come to fill their *ballas* (water jugs) at the edge of the river. (Frieze, Tomb of Ty, Saqqara, Fifth Dynasty, c. 2500 BC; modern scene on Nile bank.)

One must imagine the stepped pyramid of Zoser entirely clad with blocks of white limestone, cut according to precise angles and measures, and placed with such exactitude that their joints were most often invisible. Shimmering with light, this monument rose to more than 60 metres (200 feet) in height from within a white limestone surrounding wall of more than a mile in perimeter, whose façade was modulated with regularly spaced recesses. The funerary chamber, hollowed nearly 30 metres (about 90 feet) down into the ground below the pyramid's centre, contained the granite sarcophagus of King Zoser and gave access to rooms entirely tiled with blue ceramic tiles of indescribable beauty. Here were found the famous stelas on which Zoser executes the 'great step' marking his passage into the other world. The *earliest* known Egyptian stone building – the work of Imhotep, architect, physician and sage, who was later divinized – the Zoser complex reveals a knowledge which was never to be surpassed, nor perhaps even equalled. (Pyramid of Zoser, Saqqara, Third Dynasty, c. 2700 BC.)

The small pyramid of Unas is situated on the rocky plateau of Saqqara near the south-west corner of the Zoser complex. At the foot of a passage blocked by three granite portcullises are the funerary apartments. Their white limestone walls are entirely covered in incised hieroglyphs painted in blue, with the exception of the western area encircling the sarcophagus, which is covered in alabaster. Here the wall carving is identical with that of the mastabas of the First Dynasty, representing the tapestries thought to have decorated the pilasters and niches of their recessed walls. The ceiling, in the form of an inverted V, is covered with stars, symbolizing the destiny of the deceased to return to the breast of his mother Nut, the Sky. Life on earth is transitory; life in the other world is eternal. 'The body is for the earth, the spirit is for the sky,' affirm these, the oldest known religious texts. The subtle, immortal part of the being, enriched by its experience on earth, returns to its

Creator. But to accomplish this re-ascension the being must cleanse itself of all impurity and overcome all obstacles. It is to aid in the re-alization of this liberation that these long incantations were written. (Pyramid of Unas, Saqqara, Fifth Dynasty, c. 2400 BC.)

Compared to the lightning which passes right through space, the king hurls himself through the storm to the heights of heaven. Rê, Thoth, Horus, the Bull of the Sky, all the divine entities are implored in turn not to ignore Unas, 'who knows them', and not to thrust him aside from the 'way of stars' (probably the the Milky Way). (Pyramid Texts, 1.325–335, from the Unas Pyramid.)

The stele of the Serpent King, discovered among the tombs at Abydos, is famed for several reasons. It gives the prototype of the king's royal 'Horus-name', borne by the 'double' or *ka* modelled on the wheel at the same time as the royal child by Khnum, the divine potter of Elephantine. Every king is of divine origin; he is Horus, responsible for harmony on earth and redeemer of his father Osiris, who had been overthrown by negative cosmic forces. On this stela the falcon is perched above the representation of the palace where Horus was thought to reside. This palace is the exact replica of the superstructure of the unfired brick mastabas with façades composed of recesses and projections, characteristic of the First Dynasty, discovered at Saqqara not far from the pyramid of Zoser.

The mastaba of this same Serpent King still has its surrounding wall; and, even more remarkable, there is a second surrounding wall made up of 62 small, subsidiary tombs, each containing the remains of an individual buried in the foetal position, with the head at the north, accompanied by some vases or

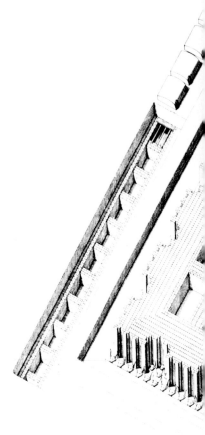

other conventional objects. Vestiges of the superstructure show evidence of 30 niches and 34 projections spread along its periphery. The structure is built on a wide platform on which, placed at regular intervals, were clay bovine heads with real horns. At the rate of 7 to each niche and 4 on the façade, there must have been a total of 346 of them. The bull played a considerable role in the Old Kingdom, and in the Pyramid Texts the King is often called 'bull of the sky'. But because of its horns the bull was also related to the moon. Thus it is tempting to note that the number of bull heads here approximates to that of 12 lunations (354 days) – and, even more closely, to the number 346.6 which Fred Hoyle, in his examination of Stonehenge, relates to the periodic return of eclipses. (Stele of the Serpent King, Djt, from Abydos, Thinite period, c. 3200 BC, Musée du Louvre, Paris; Mastaba of the Serpent King, Tomb No. 3504, Saqqara, axonometric projection and bovine heads from plinth, after Walter B. Emery, *Great Tombs of the First Dynasty*, II.)

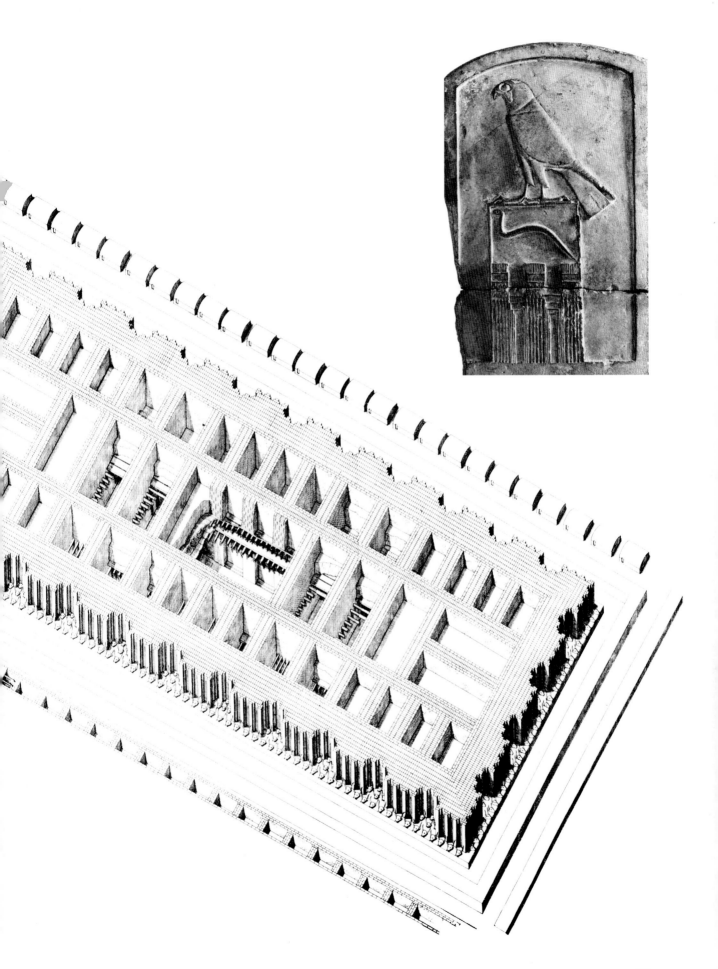

This scene of a hippopotamus hunt in the swamplands – together with some companion scenes of rowdy games among boatmen – shows an extraordinary artistic sense of movement, proportion and gesture. The creatures shown are outlined with such accuracy that naturalists can identify the species without the slightest hesitation. The crocodile is lying in wait for the fish, and one wonders why the hunters are pursuing the apparently inoffensive, herbivorous hippopotamus. The hippos are, however, the farmer's enemies: they descend on his crops in herds and wreak havoc.

In myth, the male hippopotamus is associated with Seth, enemy of light, who causes the monthly waning of the moon as well as all eclipses. At Edfu, during the yearly Feast of the Victory, Horus himself is the divine harpooner who must traverse all Egypt in his skiff in pursuit of the red hippo which is the incarnation of Seth. Ten times, at ten precise points of the body, and in ten separate locations consecrated by the legend, Horus must smite the enemy of Rê. (Hippopotamus hunt, Tomb of Mereruka, Saqqara, Sixth Dynasty, c. 2300 B C.)

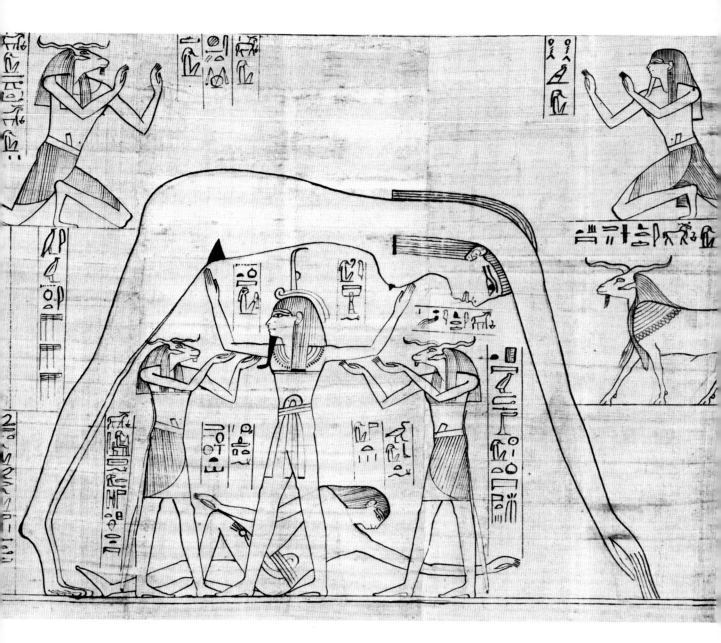

At the beginning of the world, Shu, Space, separated the Sky, Nut, from the Earth, Geb. In the Greenfield Papyrus, Nut is represented by a female figure arched forward balancing on her hands and feet in a position analogous to that of representations of the sky in the Theban tombs of the New Kingdom, lifted up and supported by the raised arms of Shu. She is thought to swallow the sun in the evening and give birth to it again at dawn, in the form of a young child.

In one of the rooms off the burial chamber of Seti I at Thebes, Nut is symbolized by a Divine Cow, emphasizing the nutritive character of the cosmic environment in which all the stars are ceaselessly regenerated. On her belly is a representation of the starry sky, and the appearance of the morning and evening solar barques at the two ends evokes the sun's daily journey. Inscribed near this celestial cow is the famous legend of the 'destruction of men' when they revolted against their Creator.

The headrest from Tut-ankh-Amun's tomb, carved from two pieces of ivory and joined together with golden pegs, represents Shu in his characteristic position of 'raising up the sky', with the sign of protection, *sa*, falling from his shoulders along his torso. The two lions framing him back to back are frequently represented in the Book of the Dead (Chapter 17) accompanied by the inscription:

'To me belongs today and I know tomorrow.
'Who is this?
'Yesterday is Osiris and tomorrow is Rê.'

(Detail of Greenfield Papyrus, British Museum, London; Celestial cow, side room of Tomb of Seti I, Valley of the Kings, Thebes, Nineteenth Dynasty, c. 1300 BC; Ivory headrest of Tut-ankh-Amun, Eighteenth Dynasty, c. 1350 BC, Cairo Museum.)

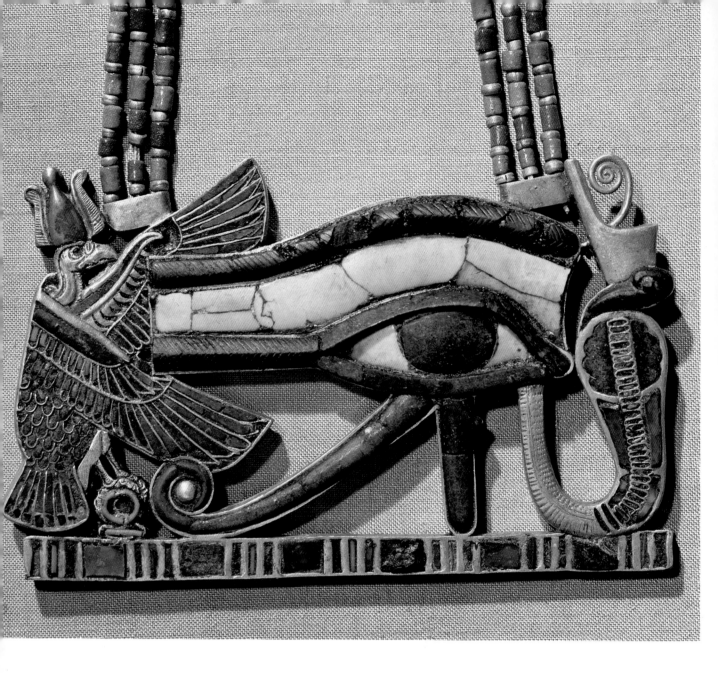

The sun and moon are the right and left Eyes of Rê, the supreme principle of light; and the following text reveals a knowledge of the true source of the moon's light: 'Khonsu-Ioh [moon], light of the night, image of the left Eye ... who rises in the east while the sun is in the west ... the left Eye receives the light of the right Eye.'

The lunar phases are symbolized in the myth by the tribulations of the left Eye of Rê, constantly under attack from Seth, enemy of Horus,

or from a black pig. It is always Thoth, Master of Time, who restores the left Eye, with which he is identified, to wholeness; another legend relates that when the sun ceases to shine at the end of the day he names a surrogate, Thoth, to make light during the night.

In one of Tut-ankh-Amun's jewels the right, solar Eye is framed by the serpent Uadjit of the north and the vulture Nekhebit of the south. These two entities, 'in the form of the two *uraei* on the king's forehead,

make the enemies tremble in their limbs'. Another of Tut-ankh-Amun's jewels shows the left Eye surmounted by a silver lunar crescent, placed on a skiff by means of which it makes its nocturnal journey. The winged scarab which seems to support the skiff represents the solar globe. These jewels are of gold encrusted with glass paste, lapis lazuli, turquoise, cornelian and chalcedony. (Jewels from the Tomb of Tut-ankh-Amun, Eighteenth Dynasty, c. 1350 BC, Cairo Museum.)

Kingly, majestic, the solar principle *par excellence,* the lion was from the beginning a symbol of the highest importance. When, 'alone in the primordial waters of the Nun' Atum, the Creator, begat himself, and 'from One became Three', the first couple to issue forth from him was Shu and Tefnut, the fiery principle of Dryness provoking the Humid, the two Primordial Lions. Then, in the Memphite myth, when the divine blacksmith Ptah (the Greek Hephaistos) actualized the creation of the world by means of the Desire of his heart and the Word of his speech, his female counterpart was Sekhmet, the lioness, the 'power-ful'. Ptah is figured robed in a straight garment from which only his hands appear, holding all the symbolic sceptres. In the Temple of Khonsu at Karnak the lioness Sekhmet is por-trayed with erect phallus, and with the solar disc encircled by the *uraeus* on her head. Her upraised arm holding the flail attracts cel-estial energy. It is therefore she who represents the catalytic action of the 'styptic fire', which concentrates and 'precipitates energy into form'.

When the Creator desired to punish humanity for its rebellion, he despatched 'his Eye' – and once again it was the lioness Sekhmet who carried out this mission of destruction. But when, placated, she returned to Egypt, she assumed a variety of names in accordance with the particular qualities venerated in different cities: Hathor, Lady of Heaven, at Dendera; Mut at Karnak, where the temple was filled with statues of Sekhmet as a human figure with the head of a lioness. (Statue of Sekhmet from Karnak, Twenty-second Dynasty, c. 930 BC, British Museum, London; Ptah with Sekhmet in ithyphallic form, Temple of Khonsu, Karnak, Nineteenth Dynasty, c. 1300 BC.)

If Egypt is the reflection of the sky, then divine beings sail on the waters of the Great River which animates the Cosmos – the Milky Way – and the deceased, in order to join this celestial fleet, must be provided with ship and steering oar.

In the temples the statues of the divine entities were kept in tabernacles placed in ceremonial barques of gold or gilded wood, of which many representations have come down to us. These were placed on altars in the sanctuaries, and the daily worship was performed in front of them. For example, the barque of Amun-Rê had the head of his sacred animal, the ram, supporting the solar disc, on both prow and poop. The ram's head rests on a lotus flower which emerges from an immense 'broad necklace' (*usekh-hat*), whose name evokes the dilation, followed by contraction, of the first creative breath. Whenever the offering of this necklace to a divinity is made, the myth of the Creation is recalled in the accompanying text, recited by the officiant in memory of the first 'inhalation-exhalation' from which the world was born.

At certain public ceremonies priests carried these barques on their shoulders to the quay, then placed them on huge ships which were drawn or towed along the river, and these processions gave rise to great rejoicing (see pp. 80–81). (Barque of Amun, Temple of Seti I, Abydos, Nineteenth Dynasty, c. 1300 BC, drawing by Amice M. Calverley.)

The myth of Osiris probably goes back to the very origins of history, for it expresses the condition, inherent in all created life, of the inescapability of death. Thus every dead person is an Osiris (since Osiris is the divine being who dies); yet all the religious texts constantly declare that the divine spark which animates man during his existence is imperishable. Osiris is therefore the principle of mortality, but also that of perpetuity: the cycles of birth, death and renewal which are observable in plant life, subject to the seasons. Each year the Mysteries of Osiris celebrate his passion, death and resurrection.

The Djed column, with its four capitals, symbolizes stability and duration in the Osirian world. Lying on the ground it expresses death, and its setting up, by the king in person, signifies the resurrection. This ceremony was a joyous one. In the Temple of Abydos the scene of the erection of the Djed column is followed by that of the Offering of Cloths, in which the column is clothed in the manner of a statue. The texts proclaim the gift of duration and of renewal to King Seti I in the guise of Horus, son of Osiris and Isis.

Osiris, seated on a throne within a *naos* or tabernacle, carries two sceptres and wears his characteristic shroud and his crown flanked by two feathers. Isis and Horus, son

of Isis, are standing behind him. The king makes the offering of Maât, held in his cupped hand. The incantation pronounced in the course of this offering is known from the Berlin Papyrus. Here is a brief extract from it:

'I have come to you, I am Thoth, my two hands united to carry Maât. ... Maât is in every place that is yours ... You rise with Maât, you live with Maât, you join your limbs to Maât, you make Maât rest on your head in order that she may take her seat on your forehead. You become young again in the sight of your daughter Maât, you live from the perfume of her dew. Maât is worn like an amulet at your throat, she rests on your chest, the divine entities reward you with Maât, for they know her wisdom ... Your right eye is Maât, your left eye is Maât ... your flesh, your members are Maât ... your food is Maât, your drink is Maât ... the breaths of your nose are Maât ... you exist because Maât exists, ... and vice versa.'

Maât is Cosmic Consciousness, the ultimate goal of Creation and of every creature, the immortal fruit of a constant acquisition. Maât is the greatest treasure that a being might wish for. (The raising of the Djed column; The king makes the offering of Maât: Temple of Seti I, Abydos, Nineteenth Dynasty, c. 1300 B.C.)

In the Temple of Abydos, in a narrow chapel consecrated to the 'Osiris-king', three pairs of scenes appear facing one another on opposite walls. The two shown here are the central ones.

On the east wall, after having received the triple sprinkling of water and of life (the 'key of life' glyph, *ankh*), the Osiris-king is standing, mummified, in the classic position holding the two sceptres in his opposed fists. Thoth, with ibis-head, gives life from his right hand, and with his left presents the two crowns of the north and the south, carried by two cobras entwined around the symbolic plants of the Two Lands. Behind the king his 'Horus-name' is inscribed above the palace between the two arms of the *ka* or 'double' glyph, placed on a shield which is itself held up by two arms, one of which holds the feather of Maât (Consciousness) and the other the staff supporting the King's 'living *ka*', an essential prerequisite of the promised rebirth. (The third tableau shows this same Osiris mummified, seated on the throne of the Sed Feast of Renewal.)

On the west wall, after having received all the sceptres in the pre-

vious tableau, the king is standing, mummified. In addition to the flail and hook he holds the long cane of Osiris along with the *uas*, sceptre of the divine entities, symbol of the flux of life. The *uas*, absolutely vertical, is placed exactly on the King's axis of equilibrium, passing just in front of the ear. It is perhaps of interest to recall that it is the semicircular canals of the inner ear that give the

sense of verticality. Notable also are the curled horns peculiar to the ram of Amun. In front of the Osiris-king, the *Iwn-Mut-f*, characterized by the braid of the crown prince and the panther skin of the officiant, performs the rite of giving incense, intended to destroy adversaries: 'the resins come, the divine perfume comes to you' (the 'perfume of the Eye of Horus', add other texts).

Isis shakes the sistrum or rattle before the divine face and holds the *menat* necklace associated with the regeneration which takes place in the following scene, where the King is represented not mummified but on the throne of the Sed Festival of Renewal. (The Osiris-king with Thoth; The Osiris-king with Isis: Temple of Seti I, Abydos, Nineteenth Dynasty, c. 1300 B.C.)

When the One wished to know himself, he first of all created himself through the projection of his heart. Then came the first breath, inspiration then expiration, dilation then contraction. He conceived the world in his spirit (*akh*), then caused his *ba* to intervene to play the role of specification, determination and animation. Thus little by little all the forms came into existence on earth, each according to its species. In the myth, each animal species concretizes a particular function – one of the steps in the genesis of total Cosmic Being.

For example, the divine entity shown as a jackal, Anubis, is charged with the embalmment of the mummy as well as the protection of one of the organs, the stomach. The jackal does indeed symbolize digestion – since not only does his keenest sense, that of smell, stimulate the secretion of the juices necessary for the transformations that foodstuffs undergo to become assimilable, but also he eats meat in a state of decomposition. Starting from the great principle that the mastery of an activity is only possible through a force of the same nature, it is then Anubis who must, through the ritual of mummification, prevent the body's corruption.

After death, the body is mummified, while the subtle parts of the being escape to follow a destiny determined by the spiritual stage reached by the dead person. The human complex includes, first of all, the *ba*, represented by the human-headed bird, often pictured fluttering about the mummy, and translated only very imperfectly by our word 'soul'. There is also the shadow, *khaibit*, written in hieroglyphs by an object which intercepts the light. This human shadow, comparable to our notion of an earthbound ghost, represents obsessions due to lower appetites remaining unappeased which risk shackling the *ba* bird, preventing its liberation.

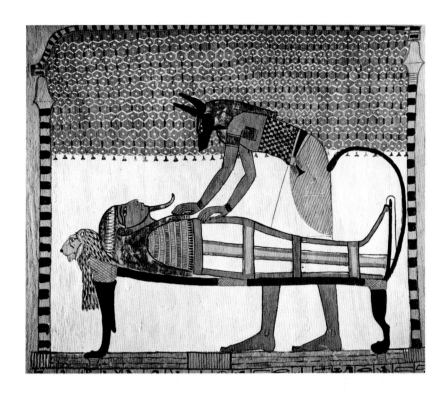

In the Book of the Coming Forth into Day, written on papyrus rolled up and placed close against every mummy, the 'Osiris-name' (the deceased) identifies himself one by one with all the Neterw, the divine entities, whom he declares that he knows. These numerous divinities are, it is written, the very limbs of God, his attributes or hypostases. Thus by virtue of the divine spark which enlivens him during his existence, the human being participates at every moment in the process of becoming conscious, in which the One, the cause of Creation, is engaged. Of the images chosen from natural phenomena to serve as symbols for these abstract notions,

one of the most typical is the daily disappearance of the sun and its rebirth in the morning. Now the sun is one of the two Eyes of the Supreme Being, and the recovery of this Eye represents, for man, the victory over all negative powers and the enrichment of his own consciousness (Maât), the ultimate goal of existence.

In a tomb in the Valley of the Queens at Thebes the mummified Osiris (left foreground) wears the feminine belt and carries the royal sceptres, for this is the tomb of Queen Nefertari, consort of Ramses II. On either side of the opening, from left to right, Selkit and Neith, divinities of the south and north,

represent the principles of contraction (the scorpion Selkit) and dilation, which make breathing (*selk*) possible. In the niches the sisters Isis and Nepthys face each other, thus completing the quartet of tutelary protective entities of the royal coffin and the four canopic vases. At the right of the door the sun, Rê-Hor-Akhty of the double horizon, sits before Hathor of the west. On the left is Khepri with the scarab as his head, symbol of the morning sun. At the very back, after having passed through the doorway framed by two representations of Maât, Consciousness, we find Osiris seated on his throne, before which are the Four Sons of Horus, protectors of

the body's four essential organs.

In this same tomb, on the back face of the wall on which Rê-Hor-akĥty and Hathor are painted, a very rare scene is found picturing a ram-headed mummy between Isis and Nepthys, accompanied by the text, 'It is Rê who rests in Osiris; it is Osiris who rests in Rê.' The few texts which refer to this scene say only, 'Secret, mystery, it is Rê, it is Osiris.' Might not this image (uniting in one figure these two great principles) be referring to the mystery of redemption, of ultimate liberation? (Interior of tomb; Detail of Rê/Osiris: Tomb of Nefertari, Valley of the Queens, Thebes, Eighteenth Dynasty, c. 1550 BC.)

The king is the 'son of Rê'. As 'king of the north and of the south, master of the two crowns' – the domains of Horus and Seth – he is felt to have mastery over antagonistic natural forces, and be capable of assuring cosmic order. The royal tombs are of an 'anthropocosmic' character. At Thebes, for example, the burial chambers of Amenophis II and Thutmosis III are painted as though a huge papyrus were unrolled around the walls on which is inscribed the Book of What is in the Dwat. This 'book' tells of the nightly journey of Rê, the Great God, through the regions of the twelve hours of the night, each of which has a gate, guardians and pilots. Voices acclaim him there saying, 'Thou livest, now, flesh, in the earth'.

Thus Rê incarnates. The name he takes when in the nocturnal barque specifies this: he is called Iwf, 'Flesh'. And by passing through these realms he animates and vivifies and regulates the phases of genesis symbolized by Khepri, the scarab: 'Come then, Rê, in thy name of living Khepri ... illumine the primordial darkness that Flesh may live and renew itself.'

Rê, then, plunges into the darkness of matter. At the Fourth Hour the serpents at the prow and poop of his boat spit flames, lighting up the secret ways. In the Fifth Hour the Great Neter presides over the metamorphosis of the scarab's egg, which has become a larva and will pass through the nymphal stage before attaining its final form of a winged insect. This mystery takes place within the sacred earth of Sokar, 'where flesh and body are found as the first phenomenal form'.

Hour after hour, phase after phase, whether imaged by the scarab's gestation or by human metabolism, the metamorphosis of the densest matter into the most volatile and subtle energy is accomplished, the return – now conscious – to the Origin. (The Book of What is in the Dwat: Fourth Hour; part of Twelfth, then Fifth and Sixth and part of Fourth Hour. Tomb of Thutmosis III, Valley of the Kings, Thebes, Eighteenth Dynasty, c. 1450 BC.)

OVERLEAF:

The king's arrival in the sky is a new birth. His mother, Nut, calls him her newborn darling. The divine entities dance attendance on him, reassemble his bones, give him back the use of his senses by opening his eyes and mouth, rituals which are accomplished magically in the 'Room of Gold' on the mummy or its effigy with two adzes and the presentation of a bull's thigh.

'O Isir! Thy mouth is opened for thee with the thigh of the Eye of Hor ... with the hook of Upual ... with this metal born of Seth, the adze of iron with which is opened the mouth of the divine entities,' say the Pyramid Texts (13–14). 'My mouth is opened by Ptah with celestial [meteoric] iron scissors', proclaims the deceased in the Book of the Coming Forth into Day (Chapter 23).

The astronomic ceilings specify that the two adzes are in fact the two constellations which we call today the two Bears, and which in the time of the building of the pyramids (when the Pole Star was Alpha Draconis) were termed 'indestructibles', that is they never disappeared below the horizon, and symbolized eternal life. But as a result of the Precession of the Equinoxes the Pole shifted, and already by the Middle Kingdom it was no longer marked by a star serving as a pivot, thus giving rise to some apprehension.

'As for this Thigh of Seth [the Great Bear], it is in the northern sky, attached to two flint stakes by a golden chain. It is entrusted to Isis, who guards it in the form of a fe-male hippopotamus' – in order that it may not depart 'into the southern sky towards the water of the gods born of Osiris, which is behind Orion'.

The Great Bear – the Thigh – is most often represented by a bovine femur. In the astronomical ceiling in the tomb of Seti I at Thebes, a bull occupies the place of the Great Bear. It is tethered by the lines and stake held by the hippopotamus. The figure standing perpendicular to this stake seems to indicate the movement of rotation undergone by the entire group. Some scholars see this figure as the constellation of the Swan, and the neighbouring figure would then be Cassiopeia. (Ceiling of Burial Chamber, Tomb of Seti I, Valley of the Kings, Thebes, Nineteenth Dynasty, c. 1300 BC.)

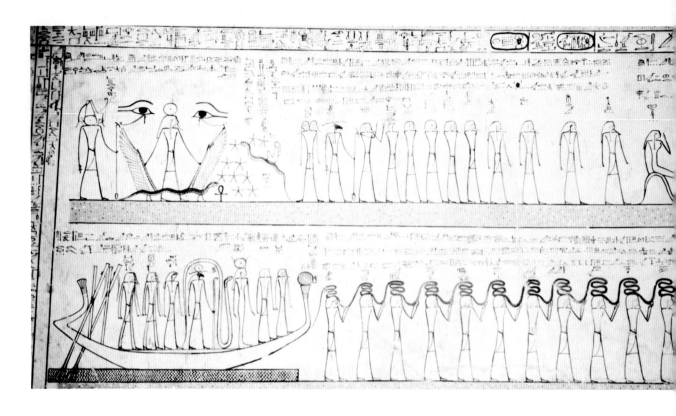

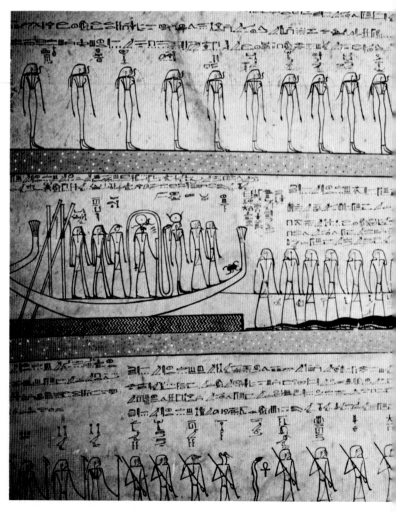

In the Book of What is in the Dwat, Iwf, the incarnation of the principle of Light, stands in the boat's cabin during the first six hours of the night, that is during the descent. For the reascent he stands in the coils of the serpent Mehen, whose name means 'spiralic', and who plays a role in the rebirth of the solar globe. Putting together teachings of the different Books, one can conceive that the sun's regeneration occurs by virtue of the flux of spiral currents which ceaselessly precipitate and coagulate the impalpable cosmic substance.

At the Eleventh Hour the regenerated solar globe is represented, for the first and only time in this Book, at the prow of the boat. The barque is drawn toward the eastern gate of the sky by the serpent Mehen, who in turn is carried on the heads of the standing figures. In the upper register a two-headed figure wears the two crowns which symbolize the union of opposites. The text – badly damaged – does not explain the winged serpent, above the two eyes which one knows are the sun and the moon, nor the small human figure seated on a serpent which takes flight through the stars, also called the Hours.

In the Twelfth Hour, in the middle register, 'This Neter sails thus in this place, into the vertebral column of this secret image of the serpent, "Divine Life", while the entities tow him. He enters in its tail and exits by its mouth, while he is born in his manifested form of Khepri [Scarab] . . .'

This is the Book's apotheosis and can be understood in several ways. Physically it is the glorious rebirth of the solar globe, and is therefore the triumph of light over darkness. Spiritually, taking into consideration the mummy lying on the ground, we can see here the sublimation of incarnate being in the image of metabolism, which, through multiple purifications, transforms the densest matter into the subtle marrow (imakh) of the spinal cord, here represented by the large serpent. The human being's spiritual quest leads him toward the state of blessedness (again imakh), and the eastern gate of the sky (at the extreme right) opens toward eternal life, the conquest of shadowless light. (The Book of What is in the Dwat: Eleventh Hour, Tomb of Amenophis II, Thebes, Eighteenth Dynasty, c. 1425 BC; Twelfth Hour, Tomb of Thutmosis III, Thebes, Eighteenth Dynasty, c. 1450 BC.)

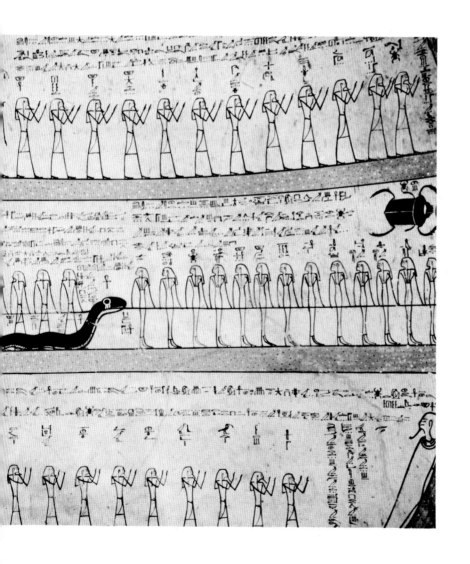

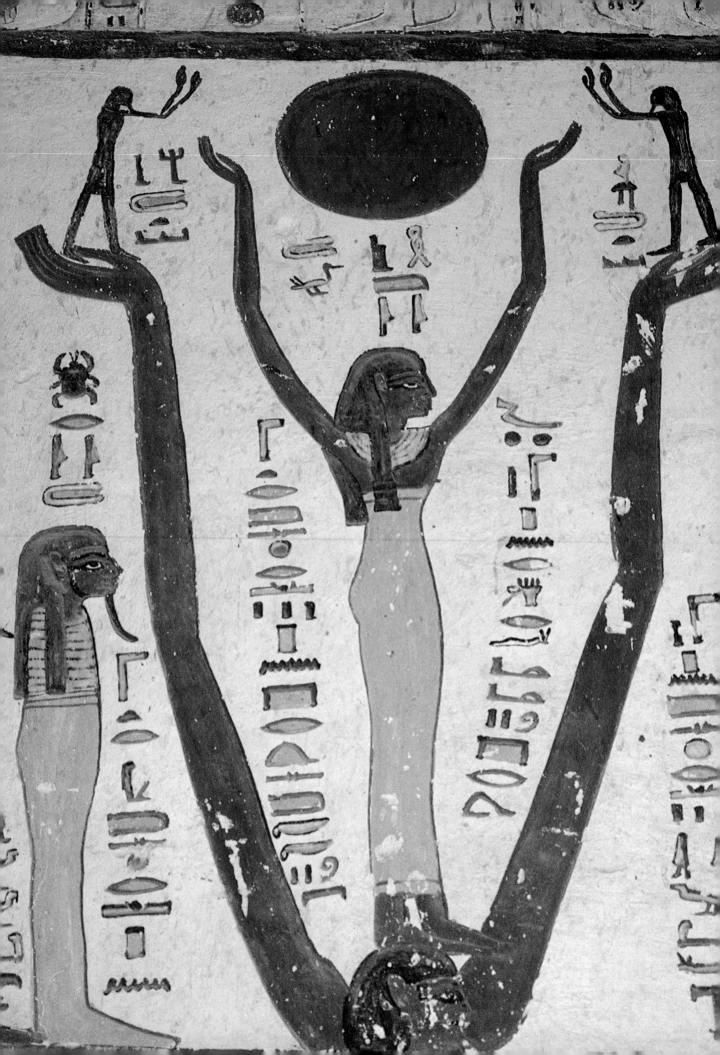

The burial chamber of the Tomb of Ramses VI is situated at the western end of galleries hollowed several hundred yards into the rock. On the north wall the mysterious Book of Aker, the entity of terrestrial powers, is represented.

According to the myth, Nut, the Sky, swallows the sun each evening and gives birth to it every morning, 'younger than it was the evening before'. It is the mystery of this regeneration that is the subject of the Book of Aker. The two middle registers, astral in character, express the different aspects of the sun's regeneration. One of these shows the coagulation of cosmic substance taking place within a funnel outlined by the coiled serpent Mehen. The arms lifting up from all sides express better than words this glorious renaissance. (Detail of north wall, burial chamber, Tomb of Ramses VI, Valley of the Kings, Thebes, Twentieth Dynasty, c. 1150 BC.)

Periods and dynasties of Egyptian history

Periods	Dates	Dynasties
Thinite period	3200–2800	First–Second
Old Kingdom	2800–2300	Third–Sixth
First intermediate period	2300–2040	Seventh–Eleventh
Middle Kingdom	2040–1800	Eleventh–Twelfth
Second intermediate period	1800–1590	Thirteenth–Seventeenth
New Kingdom	1590–330	Eighteenth–Thirty-first

Predynastic symbols

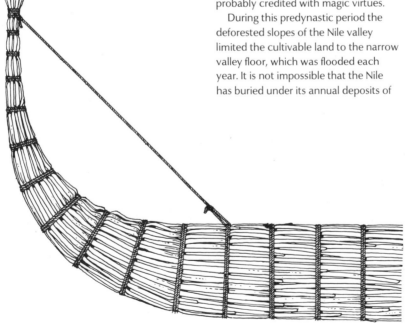

The diminishing rains on the Saharan Plateau during the Upper Palaeolithic period forced its populations – mainly nomadic hunters – into progressive migrations. Some headed south, following the climate to which they had been accustomed, while others gathered around the desert oases or along the River Nile.

Neolithic sites at the southern apex of the Nile Delta reveal the existence of a population of agriculturalists whose grain crops were carefully stored in silos. The grains of barley from these sites submitted to radiocarbon examination have been shown to date from at least 4600 BC. Long centuries of cultivation must have been necessary to develop this crop from the wild barley; it follows that the origin of agriculture, attributed to Isis and Osiris, was well before the fifth millennium BC.

Being hunters and herdsmen as well as farmers, these prehistoric peoples of the Nile valley raised cattle, sheep, goats and dogs. Their weapons, made of flint, bone or ivory, the fragments of their basketwork and cloth, and their abundant and varied ceramics, bear witness to a considerable industry. Such finds as hippopotamus bones planted in the ground and an oxhead modelled in unbaked clay suggest the existence of a cult, but it is particularly the manner of burial in the foetal position that indicates faith in survival after death and in the notion of an after-life. Some of the jewels found on the bodies of the dead have the character of amulets and were probably credited with magic virtues.

During this predynastic period the deforested slopes of the Nile valley limited the cultivable land to the narrow valley floor, which was flooded each year. It is not impossible that the Nile has buried under its annual deposits of silt a slice of history still unknown to us. Archaeologists have, however, already traced three civilizations which developed successively in the valley: the Badarian, then the Amratian, both originating in the southern part of Upper Egypt, and the Gerzean, for which the oldest sites are in the northern part of Upper Egypt. The most important sites were discovered near the locations of the provincial capitals of the historic period.

One of the most remarkable characteristics of the Gerzean is its light-coloured pottery with red figures. The principal theme of these figurations is that of many-oared boats sailing or rowing along waterways through lands which are often mountainous and peopled with a rich fauna. The form of these boats indicates that they were made of reeds. One of their two cabins, sometimes with people inside, has a mast surmounted by an ensign. The most recent opinion is that these are trading craft and their emblems indicate their home port. We can recognize in these prehistoric ensigns numerous emblems of Upper and Lower Egypt which reappear throughout the historic period. For example:

– the elephant of Elephantine at Aswan, the cow-horns of the province of Diospolis, where one of the forms of Hathor was venerated, the thunderbolt of Min of Panopolis, the falcon perched on a crescent for Hierakonpolis. If writing had not yet appeared, it was certainly already prefigured in the symbols of these ensigns.

Among the notable objects of the predynastic period, an ivory sheath of a flintstone knife from Gebel-el-Arak (Nag Hamadi) is of both artistic and ethnic interest. On one side, in mirror-image to one another (a device found as frequently in Sumerian art as in predynastic Egypt) are two attacking lions. Between them is a bearded man wearing a headdress and a long coat. Lions and costume alike recall the art of Persia and Mesopotamia. On the other side there is a combat figured above two rows of boats. The lower curved boats are of a Nilotic type, while the upper square ones are Asiatic. The combatants all wear loincloths like the ancient Libyans; but those on one side are bearded and long-haired, the others clean-shaven. Their perfectly proportioned silhouettes have been compared to figurations at Susa or at Tello.

Similarly, the workmanship and style of the earlier Gerzean vases, particularly those depicting slender-waisted, large-hipped women, also reveal a certain kinship with the painted pottery of Tepe Moussain in Elam (S.E. Iraq) and with that of Susa in Iran, the 'Sèvres' of Antiquity. Finally, in the jewellery of the period we find lapis lazuli and silver coming from Bactria and Afghanistan in Asia, and emery and obsidian from Africa, implying commercial exchanges extending from Central Asia to Ethiopia. This has given rise to the supposition that one of the trade routes was through Southern Arabia and the Red Sea, a circumstance promoting cultural interpenetration.

The theme of the King mastering his enemies is represented on a fragment of Louvre palette E 718 dating from the protodynastic period, and the name 'Bull-powerful' continues to be among the Egyptian royal titles. Here the Bull-king fells his adversaries, who have kinky or wavy hair and beards and wear as their only clothing the *karnata* or loincloth. They once more bring to mind the Libyans, of whom two races were known later on: one with brown skin and black hair, the other with blue eyes and blond hair (like the mother of Cheops). One of the faces pictures several fortresses. One of these has some writing, its name, on the interior, with the characters of a lion and a small *nw* vase. Later on the word *manw* designates the region of the western desert where the sun sets. On the other face are five emblems showing staffs, each gripped by a fist holding a cord. These are identical with the five emblems which were carried before the king throughout the historic period: the two 'Openers of the Way' from the north and the south, then Thoth, Horus and the thunderbolt of Min.

Left-hand page:

Prehistoric vase with red figures. (Ägyptisches Museum, Berlin.)

Details of two boats from a prehistoric vase. (Flinders Petrie, Q576.)

Raft made of papyrus stems. (Björn Landstrom, *Ships of the Pharaohs*, London 1970.)

Stone model of a boat made of papyrus stems. (Z.Y.Saad, *Royal Excavations at Helwan, 1945–7*, Cairo 1954, pl. 62.)

Right-hand page:

Ivory sheath of a flint knife from Gebel-el-Arak. (Musée du Louvre, Paris.)

Schist palette. (Musée du Louvre, Paris, E718.)

Mysterious origins

The predynastic remains from the Nile Valley already reveal a high degree of culture and an unquestionable seeking after perfection in craftsmanship. But nevertheless, the sudden appearance with the First Dynasty of a complete civilization utterly defies all our notions of evolution.

'There is no doubt that the ancient Egyptians were, during the First Dynasty, already highly civilized and very advanced in comparison with the other peoples of the known world of about 3200 BC. A simple glance at their constructions discovered in the excavations at Helwan [near Cairo] proves that they had attained a degree of excellence in architecture at this very early date,' wrote Zaki Y. Saad, Inspector of Excavations, in 1954 in a special issue of the *Cairo Review* dedicated to a series of great architectural discoveries which stunned the scholarly world.

In the same issue the archaeologist Walter B. Emery wrote that 'The new excavations of the Tomb of the Vizier Hemaka [at North Saqqara] led to discoveries so astonishing and so unexpected that it was finally decided to explore the entire site carefully and in detail. . . . The results of these excavations show that the civilization of the archaic period was much more advanced than had been supposed.'

The results of these excavations brought an explanation of the problem posed by the remarkable edifices in stone of the funerary complex of Zoser,

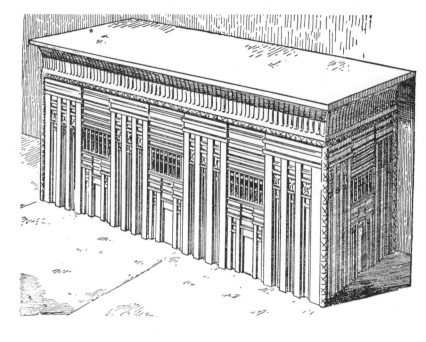

first king of the Third Dynasty. The striking variety and perfection of these vast constructions seems never to have been surpassed, even though they represent the first known attempt at architecture in stone. The study of about twenty brick structures on the plateau neighbouring the pyramid of Zoser showed for example that the surrounding wall of the Zoser complex reproduced in a large scale and in white limestone the exterior façades of the unfired brick 'mastabas' of the First Dynasty, characterized by their recessed façades.

Furthermore, vestiges of painting found on several of the mastabas, identical with the 'recessed façade' painted in the tomb of Hesy, enable us to imagine what the Saqqara necropolis was once like: about twenty edifices painted in vivid colours, each having the appearance of a sort of colossal dais with pillars or baldachins holding rich tapestries, like those one could still see in Cairo not long ago in certain religious ceremonies.

When we see these stone edifices copy brick ones, it is hard not to speculate that the latter were in turn copied from elaborate tents which had preceded them. The tent implies nomadism, and raises the perennial question of the origin of the race of the Pharaohs.

The Turin papyrus states that before the reign of King Menes, with whom the historic period is said to begin, there were venerable Companions (or Servitors) of Horus, the Shemsu-Hor, who had reigned for 13,420 years; 'reigns before the Companions of Horus, 23,200 years'. An inscription in the temple of Dendera ascribes the 'venerable organization' of worship in the city to a skin scroll dating from the epoch of the Companions of Horus. The ancients thus ascribed the art of writing, and the origins of their state, to a remote antiquity (up to 40,000 years in the past) of which we have no remains.

The basalt sarcophagus of King Menkaura or Mykerinos (left), found in the burial chamber of his pyramid at Giza, was destined to sink in 1938 near the Spanish coast with the ship carrying it to England. Thus there remain only the descriptions and drawings of it made at the time of its discovery. These, however, are of considerable value, since this sarcophagus was a scaled-down stone model of the brick mastabas of the First Dynasty, and thus makes possible a mental reconstruction of the general outline of these tombs, of which nothing remains but the lower portions.

The façades of these unfired brick buildings were composed of broad vertical piers alternating with recesses at the back of which narrow, recessed panels simulate the doors through which the deceased's *ka* (the permanent part of the being) might come and go at its pleasure. Above each 'false door' is a simulacrum of a lintel under which a roller is often found, intended for the rolled up mat or blind.

Each vertical pier is normally composed of four pilasters separated by three niches, as in the stone sarcophagus. This motif of stepped recesses caused the four façades of these ancient tombs (which are about 100 metres, over 320 feet, in length) to be animated with light and shadow. All the surfaces of the edifices were coated with plaster, whose use as an adhesive and construction material has been proven to date from prehistoric times.

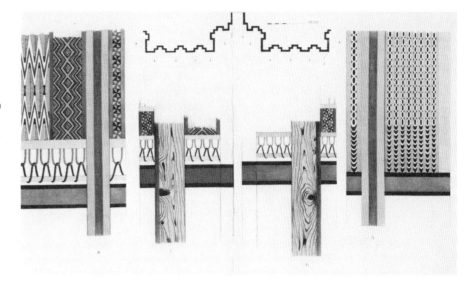

Left-hand page:

Stone sarcophagus of King Menkaura. (E.Baldwin Smith, *Egyptian Architecture*, London 1938, pl. VII.)

Part of the west façade and corridor of Tomb no. 3506, Saqqara. 'The monument can certainly be dated to the reign of Udimu.' (Walter B. Emery, *Great Tombs of the First Dynasty*, III, pl. 51a, p. p. 37.)

The theme of the façade with stepped recesses plays a very important role during the whole of Pharaonic history. We find it once more imitated in stone in the form of the 'false-door stele' for the passage of the *ka*, before which offerings were made in the Old Kingdom mortuary chapels. It is painted on the

coffins of the Middle Kingdom. It is used as a foundation for the king's 'Horus-name' during the entire historic period. The oldest known example of this Horus-name is found on the Stele of the Serpent King, King Djt of the First Dynasty (pp. 38–39).

In the Twelfth Dynasty the Horus-name stele is carried by a Nile figure, and in the Eighteenth Dynasty by the royal *ka* or double. We have already had occasion to refer to the *ka*'s strange relation with Hapy, the Nile (see p. 33).

In the oldest inscribed tomb discovered, going back to the time of Zoser, a long corridor is found whose smooth east wall is covered with paintings. The west wall is the exact copy of a stepped façade from the First Dynasty, with the difference that at the back of the eleven niches contained between the twelve pilasters there are eleven wood panels admirably sculpted with the titles and

representations of the tomb's owner, Hesy.

The pilasters represent in paint the wooden piers held together by dowelled crossbeams on which brightly coloured tapestries were hung. The geometric motifs of these tapestries evoke a particular technique: *tissage aux cartons*. On the façade of the First Dynasty tomb of King Kaa are vestiges of paintings identical to those in the tomb of Hesy.

Right-hand page:

Painted patterns in the west wall of the corridor, Tomb of Hesy, Saqqara. (J.E.Quibell, *The Tomb of Hesy*. Cairo 1911–12, pl. VIII.)

Niche of the façade of the superstructure, Tomb 3505, Saqqara, probably that of Kaa, the last king of the First Dynasty. (W.B.Emery, *Great Tombs of the First Dynasty*, III, pl. 16a, p. 5.)

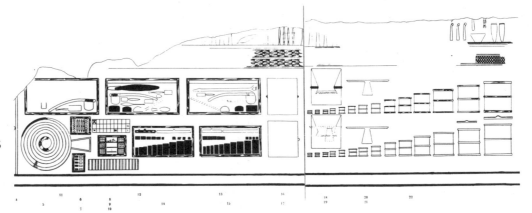

Mysterious origins

The First Dynasty royal tombs were pillaged from earliest antiquity, and only rare vestiges of their contents have been preserved. These few remains, however, bear witness to an astonishing degree of civilization.

The ceilings of burial chambers, for example, were lined with planks held up by beams which came from Byblos. This is attested by documents which furthermore reveal that a cult of the Egyptian divinity Hathor was active in that Lebanese port. The burial chamber of King Djt bears marks of the reed mats which covered its walls as well as vestiges of slender unfired brick pillars which were covered with a wood veneer, placed at regular intervals. These façades were decorated with vertical lines about a centimetre apart inlaid with fine bands of gold delicately engraved in tiny chevrons. Only a few fragments remain of this beautiful gold-braided ensemble, the tomb having been ravaged by fire at a very early date.

The many storerooms in the superstructures contained great quantities of wine jars, sealed with the name of the reigning king and an indication of the particular vineyard. Some of these vases, made of hard stone, are true masterpieces. The copper objects include a finely pointed curved needle;

board-games whose pieces, some in the form of small lions, have been recovered; and small chests inlaid with wood or incrusted with glass paste as a preservative. Implements and arms of all sorts, fragments of parade canes and sceptres, and fragments of funerary furniture – which must have been very rich if one can judge by the ivory-footed stools, gaming tables and beds painted on the east wall of the corridor of the Tomb of Hesy at Saqqara, which seems to give an inventory of the contents of these tombs.

Finally, the Third Dynasty Tomb of Hesy, an inexhaustible source of information, allows us to conclude that the measures of cylindrical capacity established on the sub-multiples of 30, 20, 10 and 64 impose the use of the cube roots of 2, 3, 5 and 10 as well as the coefficient *pi*. In addition, the standards of weights used from prehistoric times necessarily imply the knowledge of the notion of density (the relation between weight and volume).

Left-hand page:

Tomb of Hesy, east wall. Painted on this wall in life-sized figures are, from left to right: the games for which pieces have been found in the tombs along with

the small inlaid boxes in which they were kept; sets of woodworking tools, hatchet, saw, punch, identical to those in the tombs, as well as measuring rods. There is a plate on which two rulers are probably in proportion to one another as 1 to $\sqrt{5}$. They were perhaps used to calculate the small units of weight and measure numbered from 10 to 100 shown below.

The double decreasing series of the barrels, copper ones for liquids and wooden ones for cereals, is established, according to Flinders Petrie, on the decimal and binary multiples of the Pharaonic *henu* and of the Syrian *cotyle*, which is ¾ of the *henu*. The calculation of these standards necessitates the use of the cube roots of 2, 5 and 10 as well as *pi*. (J.E.Quibell, *The Tomb of Hesy*, Cairo 1911–12, pl. 16–17.)

Ivory feet of a game table or a stool found in the tomb of *Hor-Aha* and the schema for their assembly according to indications provided in the tomb of Hesy on the east wall where there is a sort of inventory of the contents of the First Dynasty tombs. In the furniture section we find pieces with the feet seen in profile and the seat seen from above. (Walter B.Emery, *The Tomb of Hor-Aha*, pl. 15b, fig. 46, pl. 18.)

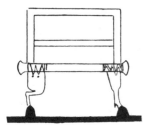 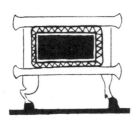  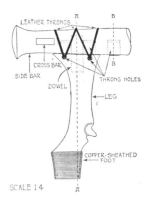

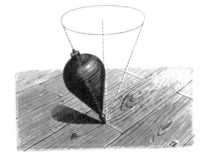

Alongside other evidence of the social and religious organization of the period, the names of First Dynasty kings were enshrined in a medical treatise and in two of the formulae of the Book of the Coming Forth into Day, of which this is one: 'This formula has been found in the foundations [of the Temple of Sokaris] by a chief mason in the time of His Majesty of Upper and Lower Egypt, Semti the Justified. It was a secret guide which had never been seen nor glimpsed.' The recitation of Chapter 64 of this Book enabled the deceased to come and go at his pleasure and assured immortality to his soul, on condition that it be read when one was pure and spotless.

Given the extreme precision brought to each detail in these First Dynasty tombs one is obliged to suppose that their proportions and measures were not made by chance. A systematic study of them indeed reveals the application of a system which was to be maintained throughout Pharaonic history. It is based on the remen, of 20 digits ($20 \times 0.01852 = 0.3704$ metres), *two* of which measure the diagonal of a square having as its side the royal cubit of 28 slightly larger digits ($28 \times 0.0187 = 0.524$ metres). The remen digit very exactly represents 1/100,000

of a minute of arc of terrestrial meridian. Its geodesic value is emphasized in vast dimensions by measurements of 1500 remen digits in the First Dynasty, and of 15,000 remen digits (277.8 metres) as the length of the perimeter wall of the Third Dynasty Zoser complex.

The use of the square root of 2 is evident in the relationship between remen and cubit; less so, perhaps, is the use of the golden section, *phi*, which underlies the geometry of a pentagon, and which is encountered at least ten times in these tombs. If we imagine in accordance with the Pyramid Texts, that the destiny of each human being is to become a star, and that a star has five points, it becomes natural to expect that the tomb must have the divine star as its geometric theme.

Archaeologists were surprised to find, in the tombs of Hemaka and Hesy, spinning discs which can only be classified as tops. They were hesitant to believe that such high officials would have amused themselves with childish games. But spinning discs and cones, as well as the earth itself, have the following 'gyrostatic' property: 'Any body turning rapidly around its axis tends to orient itself parallel to the earth's axis and its axis swings round in the same direction as the earth's revolution.'

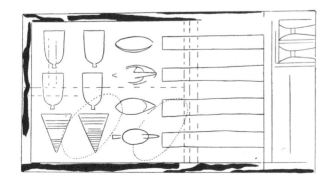

Script and symbol

Is the 'House of the Seat of Life' mentioned on one of the vases of the First Dynasty Serpent King, the prototype of the 'House of Life', the 'university' of the later dynastic period? It was in the House of Life that the young scribes learned the meaning of the hieroglyphs, mathematics, geometry, astronomy, medicine, and all that concerned the ritual and maintenance of the temples – in short, everything necessary for life on earth and in the other world.

The stone vases of the first two Dynasties, heaped in the galleries under the stepped pyramid of Zoser, along with ivory tablets and clay seals, reveal an elaborate system of administration. Writing was by this time completely constituted. This implies a long previous development; yet this development, as well as the origins of the written language, remains mysterious.

It would be tempting, for example, on the strength of certain artistic resemblances and phonetic analogies with Sumerian, which appeared at about this period, to speculate on a possible Mesopotamian origin of hieroglyphic writing. Several fundamental divergences, however, work against this hypothesis:

– while in the Akkadian cuneiform system each syllable is noted, Egyptian hieroglyphic writing (like Arabic) contains no vowels;

– as Champollion discovered, the writing is essentially composed of phonetic, alphabetic signs, consonantal signs, and determinatives specifying the nature of the object or activity, and thus has a character completely different from cuneiform.

Most of the plants and animals which are represented in the hieroglyphic writing are of southern, Nilotic origin; and Old Kingdom bas-reliefs show us that a great number of these species were imported from the regions of the Upper Nile. For example in the Tomb of Ti is a representation of transport boats above which is written 'Mooring; coming from the south'. These boats have just unloaded cranes, pigeons, hartebeestes, antelopes, caprids and/or other ruminants.

From other figurations we can see that these creatures were kept in vast aviaries and in large parks surrounded by high walls: the oldest known zoos, in which the Egyptians could study at their leisure the life and habits of the animals which they chose as symbols to figure in their writing. Each animal embodies a specific function, and it is for this reason that a particular animal was chosen as the attribute of a given divinity or of an abstract notion: a migratory bird, for example, the symbol and specific sign of *ba*, which we translate roughly as 'soul'.

These zoos are found again in the Middle Kingdom (2040–1180 BC) and in the period of Thutmosis III (1504–1450 BC) whose vizier Rekhmara receives tribesmen from the south with giraffes, monkeys and equatorial products. Hatshepsut too received the baboons which play such a great role in Egyptian symbolism because they are attributed to Thoth, master of writing and of time. For, as the Hellenistic writer Horapollo revealed, when the ancient Egyptians represented a baboon this could signify, among other things, the moon, because

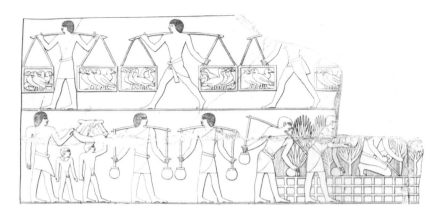

'when the moon, having entered into conjunction with the sun, is deprived of light for a fraction of a determined hour, the male baboon no longer sees nor eats. He is depressed and droops toward the ground as if he deplored the moon's abduction. . . . On the other hand, when the Egyptians wish to indicate the two equinoxes they paint a seated baboon, for at the year's equinoxes the baboon urinates twelve times in a day, that is at each hour, and also throughout these two nights. Thus it is not without reason that the Egyptians sculpted a seated baboon on their water clocks, which are made so that the water flows from its member, for as I said above, it indicates the twelve hours of the equinox.'

Left-hand page:

Cattle with a Negro whose arms are positioned like the horns of the cattle kept by the Nuer of the Bahr-el-Gebel on the White Nile. (Court of Ramses II, Temple of Luxor, Nineteenth Dynasty, c. 1300 BC.)

The earliest known zoo. Within its high walls the gazelle, oryx and wild cattle seem to live in relative liberty, since they are being hunted with hounds. (Tomb of Mereruka, Saqqara, Fifth Dynasty, c. 2400 BC.)

Right-hand page:

Even the most insignificant object of everyday use could serve to carry an abstract idea, as for example these small vases suspended at equal heights from the ends of a yoke carried on the shoulders, used by gardeners to water plants. In the hieroglyphic writing this watering device is used to express all notions of equality, and becomes the phonetic sign meaning 'similar, like', etc. (Tomb of Mereruka, Saqqara, Fifth Dynasty, c. 2400 BC.)

This scene of fishing with a net is remarkable not only for its sense of movement and balance but particularly for the precision with which the fish are drawn, permitting their exact identification. The majority of these fish, whose habits were scrupulously noted, play a role in the writing. Certain varieties of *Mormyrus,* for example (*kha*), were used as a support for a body subject to putrefaction. *Synodon* (*uhâ*), which has the habit of swimming upside-down with its belly in the air (*seben*), designates precisely this action. Even the most abstract notion can be found here, such as the idea of entering a sanctuary, or of being initiated, which is written with the fish *bes*, which hides among the rocks in the inaccessible depths of the Nile. The electric eel, well known to the ancients and represented three times in this tableau, has not yet received its phonetic attribution. (Tomb of Mereruka, Saqqara, Fifth Dynasty, c. 2400 BC.)

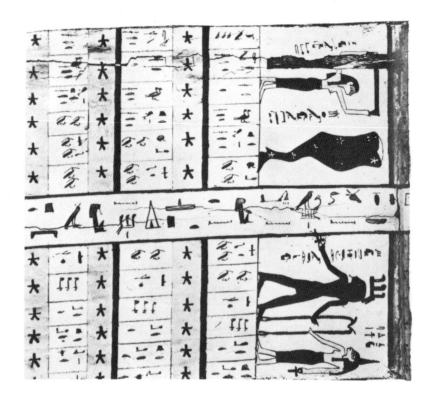

Space-time

Conceived in the image of Heaven, coffin-lids and the ceilings of sacred buildings were decorated with stars or with astronomical tables, such as that in the Ramesseum on the west bank at Thebes. In the example here, divided into three registers, the upper band is dedicated to the 36 decans and the planets, the middle band to the northern constellations and the lower band to the monthly feasts. Above the top register the 12 months are enumerated from right to left, and are divided into three seasons: inundation, seed-time and harvest-time.

Our attention is drawn to the centre of the lower register by a baboon seated on the Osirian Djed column. Sacred to Thoth, Master of Time, the baboon here recalls all cycles, whatever their duration might be: the day, defined by the earth's rotation on its axis; the year, defined by its rotation about the sun; the great year of 1460 years (see below); and finally the 26,000-year cycle of the Precession of the Equinoxes, which plays a fundamental role in the calendar. Another important cycle involved in all calendrical systems is the lunar month, which has always been a problem because it has no common measure with the other cycles.

The time contained between two passages of the sun over the meridian (north-south line) of a place is called the mean day. By consequence of the earth's movement along its orbit, the mean day is a little under 4 minutes longer than the sidereal day, which is one rotation of the earth on itself (measured by two successive passages of a given fixed star over the meridian). In the table from the Middle Kingdom, the sky is divided into 36 equal segments or decans (each of 10°), and these are enumerated from right to left, in the direction of the revolution of the earth. The horizontal lines divide the night into 12 segments of 40 minutes each; this is because the rising of each decan shifts forward by 40 minutes in a period corresponding to 1/36 of a year (just over 10 days). On these coordinates the displacement of each star is plotted, and the tables can be used to tell the time by the stars. They have consequently been given the name of diagonal star clocks.

The division of the year into 36 parts, corresponding to the decans, is made according to the decan which rises with the sun; the first begins with Sirius, whose 'heliacal rising' gives the measure of the sidereal or Siriac year, a unit of time which was known, from the very beginnings of recorded history in Egypt, to approximate to 365¼ days.

The great curiosity of the Pharaonic civil calendar, on the other hand – by which all official documents were dated – is that it used the 'vague' year of 365 days, which falls behind the Siriac cycle by one day every four years, so that the two coincide only once every 1461 vague years or 1460 Siriac cycles: the period known as a 'great year'. This discrepancy has the advantage that it enables us to date, within four years, every document mentioning both a civil and a Siriac date – such as the diagonal star clocks.

The scribes used to make jokes about the civil year, complaining that the seasons always arrived at the wrong time; but the kings had to swear an oath never to change the calendar, and it remained unaltered until Julius Caesar imposed the Julian Calendar.

The Calendar of Feasts reveals a lag in the month which started with the 'Birth of Rê', the Summer Solstice, which around the year 3300 BC coincided with the heliacal rising of Sirius. The apparent position of the sun at the equinoxes (and solstices) precesses – moves in a retrograde direction – by 50″ of arc each year, so that the tropical year, according to which all agricultural work is regulated, is shorter than the sidereal year by about 20 minutes (the length of the Julian year is between the two).

Because of this movement, known as the Precession of the Equinoxes, the earth's axis – and consequently the North Pole about which the sky appears

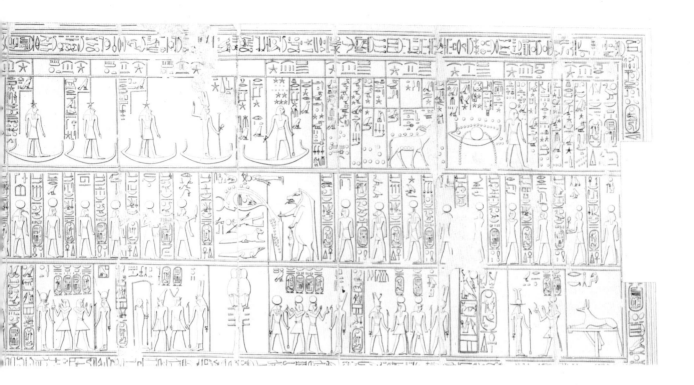

to revolve – is not fixed in relation to the stars. In a period of about 26,000 years it describes a cone, having an opening of 48°, about the stationary pole of the ecliptic. By virtue of this motion, analogous to that of a top, the Pole does not always coincide with any given star. About 2700 BC the Pole Star was Alpha Draconis, which the pyramid builders used to fix their north-south orientation with the utmost precision. But for a long period after this the Pole was empty. The observation of this gave rise to the image seen in the centre of the Ramesseum ceiling: the circumpolar constellation which we call Ursa Major, the Great Bear or the Wain, and which the Egyptians called the Thigh or the Adze; see pp. 60–61. (An adze of meteoric iron, such as was used in the funeral ritual, would of course tend to

point north-south.) Some authorities see the small falcon-headed figure who aims his spear at the Thigh as the constellation of the Swan; his spear is at an angle of approximately 48° to the vertical.

A comparison of the images of the decans shown in the Ramesseum with those in the Tomb of Senmut shows an interesting difference in the decan or segment of sky known as 'She who is at the Heart of her Barque'. In the Ramesseum, below the seven stars, there is an enormous globe from which two streams of small stars seem to issue. Might this not be a representation – the oldest known – of a supernova? This decan, the fifteenth after Sirius, is in a region of the sky near the 'galactic centre', notable for the frequent appearance of novae.

Left-hand page:

Diagonal star clock from a Middle Kingdom coffin. (O. Neugebauer and R. A. Parker, *Egyptian Astronomical Texts*, I, pl. 6.)

Right-hand page:

Astronomical ceiling, Ramesseum, (Thebes, Nineteenth Dynasty, *c.* 1300 BC.) (*The Saqqarah Expedition, Medinet Habu*, University of Chicago Oriental Institute Publications, VI, pl. 478.)

Clepsydra or waterclock of Amenophis III, *c.* 1400 BC. The external surface is laid out in exactly the same way as the later Ramesseum ceiling, which seems to be a replica of it. (L. Borchardt, *Die Geschichte der Zeitmessung und der Uhren*, pl. I, 2.)

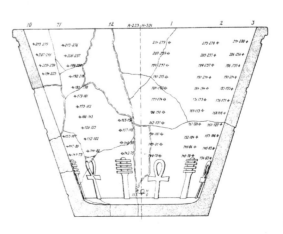

Geodesic measures

The small monument of the Sed Festival (Jubilee) of Sesostris I, who lived about 2000 BC, was demolished and its blocks reused inside the third pylon of the Temple of Karnak (built by Amenophis III in about 1400 BC). Of admirable workmanship, this small building was of the peripteral type, set on a stylobate; that is, the 16 columns which support the roof rest on a platform. Access to the platform is by means of a ramp with 8 steps.

The platform is in the form of an immense measuring-rod, similar to those preserved today in several museums. The classic type, most often made of wood and intended for actual use, is demonstrated by the Turin Museum cubit. On one of its faces is an *ascending* enumeration of digits, palms, and spans. This face is read from left to right, and the *remen* or *remen cubit* of 20 digits, the *small cubit* of 24 digits, and the *royal cubit* of 28 digits or 7 palms are all marked on it. The fractioning of each digit is read in the *opposite direction,* from 1/2 to 1/16th (= 1.17 mm or 1/22 inch). Also to be read from right to left

are the names of 28 divinities, one for each digit, from the Great Ennead to Thoth, who occupies the 15th place, appropriate for the master of measure and of time. He is preceded by the Four Sons of Horus and followed by several other entities who are also met among the northern constellations of the Ramesseum astronomical tableau (p. 75).

Some fragments of cubit measures made of basalt, and therefore too heavy to have been intended for use, seem to have been used not only as a metrical standard, but also as a compendium of

what every scribe must know. This information is found again on the small building of Sesostris:

– the list of all the provinces of Egypt, including the 22 Nomes of the south and the 16 or 20 northern ones, along with the chief town and local divinity of each;

– the surface area of each Nome, which reveals the existence of an actual territorial survey;

– the value of the local *setat,* that is to say the quantity of cubits, palms and digits that must be deducted from the *standard of 100 cubits* for each region

(an important detail which enables us to assume that nuances within the overall system were established according to geodesic data);

– the total length of Egypt (in *itrw*, a large road measure) from Elephantine, at the first cataract and thus nearly on the Tropic of Cancer, to Per-Hapi near Cairo, not far from the Nile's 'fork', and from this point to the edge of the sea at the Delta's mouth;

– the normal height of the inundation at each of these three points and the height of the inundation above the cultivated areas.

Finally, the chapel's ground plan brings a further verification of the use of the remen cubit. This measure is defined as the unit which measures the diagonal of a square whose side is measured in royal cubits. In the case of the Sesostris building,
the side = 655 cm = 350 digits of 1.872 cm = 12.5 royal cubits of 52.4 cm.
diagonal = 926.3 cm = 500 digits of 1.8526 cm = 25 remen cubits of 37.05 cm.

The diagonal of this edifice, measuring 25 remen cubits, represents 1/200th of a minute of terrestrial meridian arc at the mean latitude of 45°. This is a unit of measure already encountered in the mastabas of the First Dynasty (see p. 70). It was not necessary, then, to wait for the Greek Eratosthenes to measure segments of the meridian and thus to calculate the circumference of the earth!

The Sed Festival or royal Jubilee is represented on a door lintel found in the Temple of Medamud in Upper Egypt, containing two figures of King Sesostris III. Dressed in a straight robe from which only his hands emerge, he seems swathed or bound in the image of Osiris or of Ptah. On the right he wears the white crown of the south, while Seth, Master of the South, presents him with the symbol of the year and guarantees stability, life and power to him and his reign. In the lower corner is the divinity

Mentu, regent of Medamud, whose sacred animal is the bull. Mentu, historians note, exercised supremacy before 2000 BC (see p. 11).

On the left, robed in the same costume which is particular to the Sed Festival, the King wears the red crown of the north and receives from Horus, master of this region, the palm of years for the renewal of his reign as well as for life, strength and stability. In the left corner is the newcomer Amun, whose sacred animal is the ram. Amun confirms the gifts of Horus.

In the upper corners we find Horus again on the left facing the pavilion of the north, perched on the symbol of the inundation and consequently of renewal, and on the right is the Benu bird which here replaces Thoth or his ibis (which itself often takes the place of Seth).

This ritual is certainly very ancient since it is found on many Thinite, First Dynasty, and even predynastic documents. Spiritually it is concerned with a rebirth, simulated by the 'passage through the amniotic sac', here recalled by the straight, enclosing robe. This robe evokes at the same time the mummy and the metamorphoses which take place mysteriously during the nymphal phase of the Lepidoptera.

Under the cornice our attention is

drawn to a gargoyle, a spout in the form of a lion's head – a surprising feature, since it practically never rains in Upper Egypt. This brings to mind something Plutarch says in *Isis and Osiris*, Chapter 38: 'Among the stars Sirius is the one attributed by the Egyptians to Isis because it leads forth the water. They also revere the Lion, and they ornament the temple doors with gaping lion mouths [and] . . . cause their fountains to spring from lion mouths, because the Nile spreads its new waters over the seeded lands of Egypt at the period in which the sun passes through the sign of the Lion.'

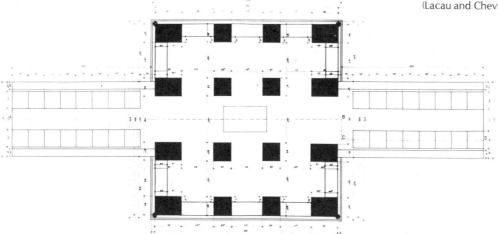

Genesis and number

According to the myth as recounted at Heliopolis, Atum, the Self-Creator, was alone in the Nun, the cosmic ocean, at the time of the original creative impulse. Because of its role in the creative act (see p. 9), Atum's hand was divinized as 'the hand of Atum which gave birth to Shu and Tefnut'. Unnamed at first, it was later shown in the form of two female divinities, Iusaas, mistress of the sky, and Nebet-Hetepet, mistress of the sky, sovereign of the gods. These two were assimilated in their turn to Hathor, the sky, the cosmic milieu, as well as to Mut, the feminine principle and counterpart of the Theban Amun.

In a bas-relief in the Temple of Medinet Habu at Thebes, King Ramses III receives the royal emblem from Atum and is followed by Sechat, divinity of writing, who inscribes numerous re-newals and Jubilees for him. In the great Temple of Karnak, also at Thebes, where the triad Amun, Mut and Khonsu was venerated, an inscription on the portal associates Thebes with the original place of the Creation.

The famous hymn of Leiden Papyrus I, 350 (see p. 13) not only confirms this but casts light on the relationship between this place and the generative principles symbolized through number. It was probably conceived with 27 stanzas, numbered from 1 to 9, then from 10 to 90 in tens, then from 100 to 900 in hundreds; only 21 have been preserved. The first word of each is a sort of pun on the number concerned. Thus, stanzas 10 and 100 (1 is missing) are concerned with the Creation, the First Time:

Stanza 10: 'Thebes, more exact than any other city; whose water and earth date from the first time. . . .'

Stanza 100: 'He who began the be-becoming the first time. Amun who became at the beginning, whose mys-terious emergence is unknown. No Neter had come before him who could reveal his form. His mother who made his name does not exist. A father who could say, "I engendered him" does not exist. It was he who hatched his own egg. Powerful, mysterious of birth, creator of his "sexual power". God of Gods, who came from himself. All the divine entities became after he com-menced himself.'

Stanzas 20 and 200 evoke the dual nature of Hor-Akhty, the solar principle of the double horizon, whose course creates the years, months, days, nights and hours, and who becomes 'younger each day than the evening before'. The contrast is here evoked between the bursting forth of the sun's apparent form and the mysteries of its obscure metamorphoses. Amun is assimilated by turns to Atum with whom he forms but a single body, to Rê as the 'Gold which is in Heliopolis', to Ta-Tenenn (Ptah), the primordial hill which emerged from the Nun. Then the sacred character of the One, the inaccessible, is stressed at length: 'His image can never be drawn, nothing can be taught of him, for he is too mysterious for his secret to be unveiled, too great and too powerful to be approached . . . one would fall dead at once if one dared to pronounce his secret name, consciously or unconsciously.'

Stanza 30 has a curious and un-expected play on the words 'thirty' and 'harpoon', which are written in exactly the same way. A passage of the Pyramid Texts (1212) describes this weapon thus: 'the harpoon [thirty] . . . whose handle resembles the [celestial] waters and whose barbs are the thunderbolts of Rê'. In the

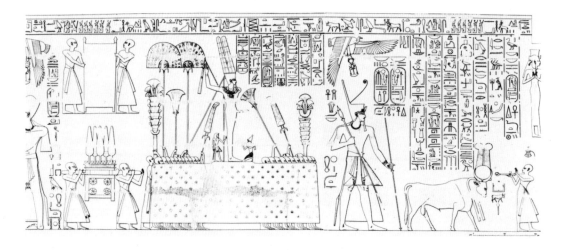

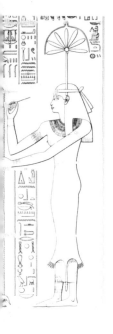

hymn it is by virtue of this weapon, the harpoon, that the solar barque masters storm, thunder and the elements, a power also accorded to the 'hand of Atum' in certain magical texts.

Stanza 300 declares the unity in one Being of the three principles, Amun, Rê and Ptah, whose cities, 'established for ever', are Thebes, Heliopolis and Memphis. This statement constitutes firm evidence against both the argument for polytheism and the notion of 'rivalries' between the different cult centres.

Stanza 40 introduces the 'Becoming', telling of the mysterious craftsman (*hm*) of the origin. The number 40 (*hm*) is traditionally related to genesis, on the physical as well as on the spiritual plane. In this stanza, 'The imperceptible essence creates itself' by its own energy, in order to 'cause its egg to become', thus signalling the beginning of the phase of physical genesis.

In Stanza 400 is found Ka-Mut-f, 'bull of his mother', who 'gives birth to that which is and that which is not', as the 'father of fathers, the mother of mothers'. He is the ithyphallic Min-Amun whose procession is figured at Medinet Habu.

Stanzas 50 and 500, whose first word *dua* means at the same time 'five' and 'to worship', consist of magnificent hymns of adoration exalting the marvels of the Creation.

Stanza 6 is the first which remains intact of the unit series of numbers 1–9. Because of the six directions, 6 is the

number *par excellence* of space, volume and time, and thus this stanza deals with all the regions which are under the dominion of Amun-Rê, from the River Euphrates to the land of Punt in Somalia (not forgetting the Greek archipelago) and their products: gums, resins, wood, minerals (gold, silver, copper), lapis lazuli, turquoise; in short, all that was necessary for the temple and its ritual.

In Stanza 60, Amun not only governs the entire earth but his power extends to the edges of the Universe. He controls the land survey, the cubit and the measuring cord, as well as the foundation of temples.

Stanza 600 says of Amun:

> Sia, Knowledge, is his heart,
> Hu, the Word, is his lips,
> His *ka* is everything that exists by
>   virtue of his tongue.
> His soul (*ba*) is Shu, the air, his
>   heart is Tefnut, the fire.
> He is the Horus of the double
>   horizon who is in the sky,
> His right Eye is the day, his left the
>   night.
> He is everyone's guide in all
>   directions,
> His body is Nun ... he gives birth
>   to everything that is and
>   causes all that exists to live. . . .

Stanza 7, 70 and 700 are directly related through the number 7 (*sefekht*) to Sechat-Sefekht, the divinity of writing who wears a seven-rayed emblem on her head. The number 7 constantly comes into magical prescriptions and incantations, and these stanzas are

themselves related to deliverance from ill-fortune, adversity and sickness.

Stanza 80 retraces the Creation as told in the Hermopolitan myth which deals with the Ogdoad, the Primordial Eight, who comprised the first metamorphosis of Rê-Amun, the mysterious, hidden one who became in turn Ta-Tenenn of Memphis, then Ka-Mut-f of Thebes, 'bull of his mother', yet all the while remaining One.

Stanza 9 recalls, obviously enough, the Great Ennead, the first nine entities which came forth from the Nun. They are here brought together in Amun who is merged into them and raised up into a 'golden sky', while the 'Nun is of lapis lazuli and the earth dusted with turquoise'.

Left-hand page:

Atum, Iwsas and Nebet-hetepet, his hand divinized, in the *naos*. (*The Temple of Medinet Habu,* University of Chicago Oriental Institute Publications, V, pl. 295.)

Min-Amun on litter in procession, preceded by the King and the sacred white bull. (Ibid., IV, pl. 196.)

Right-hand page:

Ramses III offers sacks of gold and lapis-lazuli along with precious gums from foreign countries to the ram-headed Amun-Rê. (Ibid., V, pl. 238.)

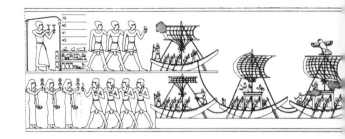

Hathor of Dendera and Horus of Edfu

Horus the Elder (as distinguished from Horus the Child, son of Isis) was venerated particularly at Edfu as the divinity of light triumphant over Seth, entity of darkness. Horus of Edfu, then, as the principle of light, is represented by a solar globe with the wings of a falcon, his sacred animal. On the inner face of the east pylon of the Temple of Edfu is a minutely detailed description of the annual Festival of the Reunion, in the course of which Hathor of Dendera (of lunar character) was brought to Edfu to meet Horus at the new moon, to celebrate the day of the conjunction. So rich in detail are the Edfu texts that they enable us to reconstruct this happy festival just as it must have happened. The following is an evocative summary of these texts.

Excitement pervaded Dendera, Hathor's city, starting on the 4th of the month of Epiphi, and festivities followed one another practically without interruption. Most of these ceremonies, however, were enacted within the surrounding walls of the Temple, and the population heard only vague echoes of them. The following weeks were awaited with feverish impatience, for it was then that the Beautiful Sailing of Hathor, the great annual voyage, would take place, and the rite of the first fruits of the field would be celebrated 'in conformity with the edicts of Amenemhet'. (The fact that Amenemhet, a king of the Middle Kingdom, is mentioned here indicates that the ritual goes back at least to 2000 BC.)

In anticipation of the great celebration, inhabitants not only from the neighbouring province of Diospolis Parva, but also from the desert oases, camped here and there along the banks of the river. It was very hot, and already one could see that the Nile was rising.

At last the day arrived, four days before the new moon of Epiphi. The gate of the temple courtyard slowly opened and the four doorkeepers emerged. Then came the steward to the temple stores and the bearers of the fire-altars, followed by the three treasurers. Next came the Priests of the Hours, the Pure Priests, the Prophets, and the Priests of the Sacred Writing. Finally, and very slowly, the bearers of the sacred emblems appeared, and then, walking backwards, came several priests burning incense which billowed out into the surrounding air. It was thus as from behind a light veil that the small golden barque containing the divine *naos*, the tabernacle, appeared, carried on the shoulders of priests dressed in great robes of starched linen.

It was She! Hathor, the Eye of Rê, the Golden One! Rapt in awe and emotion, the people contemplated the procession as it moved silently towards the river. The golden barque took its place in the great barge, *Mistress of Love*, whose bow and stern were decorated with Hathor's effigy. This vessel was towed by five others. Each took its place according to an established order: the first held the king's steward, the second, with a falcon flying above it, carried the treasurer along with the choir from Hierakonpolis (Nekhen) accompanying the statue of Horus of Nekhen who had come to seek the divine Hathor. Into the third climbed the mayor of Edfu and more singers. The remaining dignitaries took their places in the other boats.

On each bank, in long parallel ranks, were the soldiers of the army, each with his weapon. They were accompanied by the young men from the town and countryside, each brandishing a leafy tree-branch and preparing himself to undertake the long journey accompanying the boats. The day's journey was to be made in a single stage, for the first stopping-place was 60 kilometres (37 miles) upstream. Other pilgrims prepared themselves to follow, some on foot, others in small boats.

Each person on board had his own defined role. The Nomarch or governor of Elephantine and his retinue had to oversee the 'opening of the waters' (the constant sounding of the water's depth, essential to avoid running aground on the sand-banks, so frequent in the Nile), while the vizier of Dendera and his company kept constant watch. The mayor of Hierakonpolis held the cable at the bow, the vizier of Komir held the one at the stern, and these two cities also provided the crews of the guide boats.

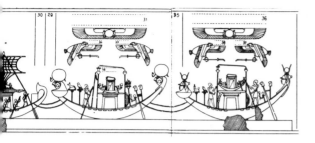

The first stopping place was an important one, and it was necessary to arrive early. On entering the eminent province of the Great Nun (Karnak), the entire retinue was to go ashore. It would then form a procession, for Hathor had to make a tour of the Temple of Mut which was half-encircled by the Lake of Asheru in the form of a lunar crescent. It was here that innumerable statues of Sekhmet, the bloodthirsty lioness, were found, and homage had to be rendered since Sekhmet is an aspect of Hathor in her form of the Eye of Rê.

The legend recounts that at the origin of time, men conspired against their Creator. After considering the matter, Rê decided to send his Eye in the form of a lioness, Sekhmet ('powerful'), to chastise the insurgents. Sekhmet wrought havoc and would have devoured all humanity had not Rê, stricken with regret, then had the ground covered with red-dyed beer in place of blood, so that Sekhmet, deceived by the colour, drank up the liquid, became drunk and fell asleep, thus sparing mankind. This took place, however, very far to the south of Egypt. It fell to Thoth, disguised as a monkey, to bring Sekhmet back into Egypt. Barely had the two arrived in Aswan, however, when Thoth plunged her into the waters of the Abaton in order to 'quench her heat'. And thus it was that the bloodthirsty lioness was transformed into the gentle cat, Bastet, one of the aspects of Isis-Hathor.

There were 70 kilometres (44 miles) to cover on the second day in order to arrive at Komir, the next stopping place. Here bread, beer and all sorts of good and provisions were brought aboard for the pilgrims and participants in the festivities.

The third stop was Hierakonpolis Nekhen, the ancient metropolis of the southern kingdom, where the sacrificial ox was obtained. The day's journey was only 20 kilometres (13 miles), undoubtedly in order to allow for some rest, since the following day's voyage was to be extremely charged with ceremonies of all sorts.

Only 19 kilometres (12 miles) remained to be covered before reaching Edfu, the goal of the journey, and it was necessary to arrive there at the 8th hour of the day (2 p.m.). But before this, at a certain distance from the town, the great ceremonial barge of Edfu was to appear, its prow and poop ornamented with a falcon's head surmounted by a solar disc. It had to come to meet the divine Hathor at a place called the 'seat of Horus' and take its place in the procession. Here various ceremonies were enacted and a sort of augury was taken. Before the procession could continue on its route to Edfu, four geese, standing for the Four Sons of Horus, had to fly towards the four cardinal points, as in the coronation ritual. If they did not, there was an 'obstacle' or unfavourable omen, and it was necessary to 'lower the masts, pull in the mr.t chests (the ritual cloths), strike the cattle, bow, offer Maât, raise up the offering dishes, while the musicians [those-who-beat-the-measure] present bouquets of jujube and willow … in the presence of Neith-who-opens-the-waters-and-the-banks'.

This accomplished, the procession moved on to the Mound of Geb (Earth), where new offerings were made, before finally arriving at the landing wharf of the great Temple of Edfu, where the vessels pulled alongside the bank exactly at the appointed hour on the day of the new moon.

There was an explosion of sound from all directions. Shouts and tambourines echoed through the town and countryside: 'Joy for ever! Joy for ever!' Menats, sistrums and crotalums vibrated noisily, while the priests took the provisions from the vessels and distributed them 'so that the villagers might have happy festival days and rub themselves with unguents', and of course sing, dance and make merry. In the court of the Temple of Edfu, singers, musicians, harpists and dancers waited while the divine barques, preceded by their emblems, were carried off the ships and placed at last in their repositories in the temple. The Hymn to the Golden One (see p. 82) was sung: Horus and Hathor were united.

The ceremonies lasted thirteen days. On the morning of the fourteenth the procession re-formed, the ships returned downstream amid the acclamations of the crowd. Led by the helmsman, the rowers chanted to the rhythm of their oars.

Left-hand page:

Façade of the Temple of Dendera. (Emile Chassinat, *Le Temple de Dendera*, Cairo, Institut français d'archéologie orientale, 1935, I, pl. 21.)

The river procession. (Emile Chassinat, *Le Temple d'Edfu*, Cairo, Institut français d'archéologie orientale, 1960, X, pl. 126.)

Courtyard of the Temple of Edfu showing a portion of the back of the pylon on which the Festival of the Reunion is described.

Right-hand page:

The barques containing figures of Horus and Hathor placed in their repositories in the Temple of Edfu. (Emile Chassinat, *Le Temple d'Edfu*, Cairo 1960, X, pl. 127.)

Hymn to Hathor

All hail, Jubilation to you, O Golden One,
Sole ruler, Uraeus of the Supreme Lord himself!
Mysterious one who gives birth to the divine entities,
    forms the animals, models them as she pleases,
    fashions men . . .
O Mother! . . . Luminous One who thrusts back the
    darkness, who illuminates every human
    creature with her rays,
Hail, Great One of many names . . .
You from whom the divine entities come forth in this
    your name of Mut-Isis!
You-who-cause the throat to breathe, daughter of
    Rê, whom he spat forth from his mouth in this
    your name of Tefnut!
O Neith who appeared in your barque in this your
    name of Mut!
O Venerable Mother, you who subdue your
    adversaries in this your name of Nekhebet!
O You-who-know-how-to-make-right-use-of-the-
    heart, you who triumph over your enemies in
    this your name of Sekhmet!
It is the Golden One . . . the lady of drunkenness, of
    music, of dance, of frankincense, of the crown,
    of young women, whom men acclaim because
    they love her!
It is the Gold of the divine entities, who comes forth at
    her season, in the month of Epiphi, the day of the
    new moon, at the festival of 'She is Delivered' . . .
Heaven makes merry, the earth is full of gladness,
    the Castle of Horus rejoices.
(Translation after M. Alliot, *Le Culte d'Horus à Edfou*,
    pp. 491 sqq.)

Under the multiple names which evoke her countless aspects, Hathor represents a synthesis of all notions concerning cosmogenesis, and as such she is of much greater universality than Aphrodite, with whom the Greeks identified her. Despite her female epithets, however, we must guard against considering her exclusively as the Feminine Principle; under the name of Neith she is addressed as 'Lady of Sais, that is to say Tanen, two-thirds masculine and one third feminine' (Serge Sauneron, *Esna*, V, 100).

In this aspect Neith takes the role of the Creator surging forth from the initial waters. Everything that her heart conceived, became, at that very moment, realized. *Seven propositions* issued successively from her mouth, and these seven propositions became *seven divine beings*. Thus began the genesis of the world which she, in the form of a cow, meditated, from the moment of her own creation to the creation of man: 'For all creatures came into existence after she was born. It is she who touches the boundaries of the entire universe under her bodily aspect of surface liquid, and under her real nature of unlimited time' (Serge Sauneron, *Esna*, V, 280).

Neith-Hathor is the totality of the cosmos, indeed space-time itself. In this aspect, the divine cow Neith-Hathor takes the name Mehet-wrt. This can be translated as 'great-full' in the sense of the inexhaustible cosmic source, but it also means 'great swimmer' since the legend tells us that Mehet-wrt, after having given birth to the solar globe, carried it between her horns as she swam in the cosmic ocean. But this does not prevent the myth from asserting that Hathor's son is the falcon Horus, also called Rê-Hor-Akhty, the solar principle of the double horizon.

Mehet-wrt is figured in cow form with the sky as her belly, in which the stars move (p. 45). She is also represented lying down, draped in a cloth – usually red – covered with a network of pearls. Around her neck she wears the *menat* necklace, particularly associated with Hathor, and its counterpoise rests on her spine. On a sarcophagus from the time of Ramses II (c. 1250 BC), Mehet-wrt bears the flail of Min over her haunches, and Rê-Hor-Akhty is found in front of her hoofs. The caption written above this tableau reads: 'The falcon Horus who rises up in the Nun, Lord of Mehet-wrt'.

The *menat* necklace and its counterpoise play a considerable part in temple and funerary ritual, where they are related to notions of birth, rebirth or the passage to a new state. The *menat* can be seen, for example, around the neck of Isis-Hathor as she leads Queen Nefertari toward the throne of Osiris. According to the inscription above the presentation of the *menat* and sistrums to Ramose by three priestesses of Amun, these objects endow the deceased with 'The persistence of life, durability, ever-renewed youth'. This *menat* necklace is presented by female divinities, who take their

name from it, both to the royal child and to the king at his Sed Festival or Jubilee. And in the Temple of Dendera, called 'Castle of the Menat', this piece of jewellery even becomes anthropomorphized.

Hathor as the nourishing principle is figured in the form of a cow suckling the royal prince. Every new-born child destined for the throne is assimilated to Horus, Son of Isis, posthumously begotten by Osiris. Isis, fearing the misdeeds of Seth, nursed her child in great secret in the Delta swamps. This is why we find, for example, a cow in a papyrus thicket on the rounded part of the counterpoise of the *menat* necklace, the rest of which represents Isis-Hathor.

Hathor comprises in herself the Seven Hathors who fix the destiny of the new-born child, or again the 'seven celestial cows' which can be related to the seven notes of the scale, the seven colours, etc. She is omnipresent, being worshipped as much at Byblos in Lebanon as at Punt in Somalia, or in the turquoise mines of Sinai.

Left-hand page:

Isis-Hathor. Tomb of Nefertari, Thebes, c. 1250 BC.

Mehet-wrt as cow. Sarcophagus of Khonsu, c. 1250 BC. (Cairo Museum, no. 27302.)

Right-hand page:

Women with sistrums and *menat*. Tomb of Ramose, Thebes, c. 1350 BC.

Hathor as cow suckling a man. From Temple of Hatshepsut, Dier-el-Bahari, c. 1450 BC. (Cairo Museum.)

Seven celestial cows and bull. Tomb of Nefertari, Thebes, c. 1250 BC.

Music and cosmic harmony

By means of various flutes and other instruments that have been recovered, and by the many representations of musical scenes pictured in the tombs of noblemen from all periods, we know that from the Old Kingdom onwards the Egyptians utilized musical scales analogous to our own. The positions of the harpists' hands on the strings clearly indicate ratios such as the fourth, the fifth and the octave, revealing an unquestionable knowledge of the laws governing musical harmony. There was no written music, but singers made use o a hand-language which indicated to the instrumentalists the notes or chords to be played. This method, called chironomy, was still in use in Egypt until the middle of this century.

Hathor is identified with Maât, principle of order, equilibrium and cosmic harmony. Thus Maât is found not only in the innermost sanctuary of the temple but also as the decoration on a harp. In the epithets of the hymn to Hathor on p. 82, 'lady of drunkenness, lady of music', the word *tkh*, here translated by 'drunkenness', designates above all else the weight suspended by a string from the end of the feather which symbolizes Maât in representations of a pair of scales. This plumb bob, *tkh*, determines the vertical and governs the equilibrium of the scales. Scenes of weighing show that it is necessary to still the plumbline, because otherwise it would continue to oscillate. The word *tkh* is accordingly also used to express everything that oscillates, titubates, or, by extension, wobbles – as in drunkenness. Furthermore, vibration being but a rapid oscillation, the word *tkh* can remind us that every vibrating body emits a sound. This is in fact what is suggested by the sistrums, crotalums and *menats* agitated by the officiants in religious ceremonies, or by the strings plucked by musicians.

The plumb bob *tkh* is very often modelled in the form of a heart, *ib*, 'the dancer'. The heartbeat provides us with a convenient measure of time; and as the rate of oscillation of a pendulum varies in inverse ratio to the square of its length, it is possible to determine the length of a plumbline which will swing in the rhythm of an average heartbeat; this is 0.69 metres or about 27 inches.

This law, which results from the phenomenon of universal gravitation, constitutes the essential basis of musical harmony, one of the direct applications of which is the length of a harp string. The longest string emits a sound of a certain pitch. Half this length emits a sound consisting of vibrations twice as rapid as the first, and one octave higher. Thus all the intervals which define the seven notes of the diatonic major scale represent ratios betwen 1:1 and 1:2, and the relationship between the string-lengths for any two notes is the inverse of the relationship between their rates of vibration. For example, for the fifth, such as C to G: the ratio between the two rates of vibration is 2:3 (260:390 Hertz), and that between the two string lengths required on any given instrument is 3:2.

Thus the oscillation of the plumb bob leads to the profound laws ruling the genesis of the cosmos, the first heartbeat, the first breath, the polarization of energy which unleashes the entire vital process, the concretization of the state which is latent in the immensity of the Nun.

In the sanctuary of the *menat* in the Temple of Dendera, a pedestal or stand is figured on the south wall whose

proportions, expressed in palms, are 8 : 9, the musical ratio of a whole tone. On this stand rests the counterpoise of the *menat* necklace which terminates in a bust of Hathor. She presents keys of life (*ankh* symbols), which she holds in her hands, and one of her arms supports the divine Child Horus. Before her sits another Hathor, who displays the *menat* in one hand while the other holds a crotalum, her particular emblem, in the presence of the small figure of Ihy, harmony.

On the north wall, facing this scene, is shown the great *usekh* (the 'broad pectoral'), which in the ritual of daily worship is always related to the initial coagulation, the effect of the first alternation of dilation and contraction at the origins of the world. The counterpoise is standing up near the *usekh* itself, to which it is joined by four strings of pearls attached to four crotalums. The latter are very important symbols since they are used as capitals for the columns in the Hypostyle Hall. The crotalum is a percussion instrument consisting of a cubic resonator and two long arms ending in lateral spirals. These spirals recall the cochlea of the inner ear, which enables us to hear and to distinguish different pitches. The cubic shape evokes the three semicircular canals of the inner ear by virtue of which we have the sense of three directions in space, i.e. of volume. The word *tkh*, the plumb bob, reminds us that these canals also give us the inner sense of equilibrium and verticality.

The synthesis of cosmic genesis is evoked by the representation of Iwsas-Nebet-Hetepet 'the divine hand of the Self-Creator, Atum', framed by two columns, each surmounted by a temple-shaped crotalum. On the lower part of this counterpoise, Hathor's head with its cow's ears resting on its emblem is placed over the sign for gold, and it is framed by two cats, themselves wearing the counterpoise at the neck.

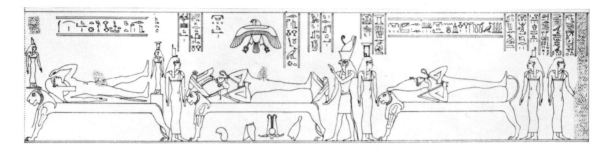

Death and metamorphosis

The Mysteries of Osiris

If there were Mysteries in Egypt they were certainly those of Osiris. Alexandre Moret notes in his book *Mystères égyptiens* that the classical writers concur in acknowledging their existence, but also in not discussing them. According to the information provided by the Pharaonic buildings themselves, it would seem that there were two categories of Mysteries, as we use the word. On one hand there were 'mystery plays', performed in public like those in our Middle Ages, and on the other, certain secret rites revealed only to initiates prepared to know them, and of which nothing, consequently, has come down to us.

From the representations we have of the more public Mysteries, it can be concluded that their fundamental theme is that of the permanence of life, even in face of the death inherent in every creature: there is no ultimate death, but only changes of state throughout an ever-renewing genesis from seed to the fruit which is the new

seed. When the king himself cut the sheaves with his golden sickle in the harvest season it represented the death of Osiris. The threshing evokes his dismemberment by Seth, while the sowing is his entombment, and at the same time the posthumous fecundation of Isis (the earth) by Osiris (the grain).

The decomposition and processes of metamorphosis which occur 'mysteriously' in the earth's breast were probably attributed to Ptah-Sokar: in the Book of What is in the Dwat it is in Sokar's 'mound', in 'the secret of darkness', that the scarab's egg is transformed into worm or larva in preparation for the nymphal phase. In the plant kingdom, as in the animal kingdom, the new germ appears only after the total destruction of the previous form. Here there is polarization, in the sense that the shoot grows upward searching for light while the root drives downward into the darkness of the earth.

Attached to germination is the idea of rebirth or resurrection. In the Osiris legend this is evoked primarily by the erection of the Djed column, which quite probably took place as a public ritual. This pillar has four capitals often surmounted by a disc, feathers, or a

crown. When it is lying on the ground, it represents the dead Osiris. Its erection symbolizes his resurrection.

According to a document which is now lost, and of which only a sketchy summary remains, the priests and the king together pulled on the twin hawsers to raise the Djed column, while the people, divided into two clans, the partisans of Osiris and those of Seth, mimed a pitched battle. The suitable outcome, of course, was for the partisans of Osiris to win, expressing victory over death through resurrection.

This festival of the renewal of life clearly appears in the ritual of the royal Sed Festival or Jubilee, during which the king passes through an animal skin and curls up in the position of the foetus in the womb, as if he were being gestated once more in the belly of his mother Nut, the sky, in the likeness of each day's sun.

This animal skin (later replaced by a close-fitting robe) was called by different names constructed on the word 'to be born', and assimilated to 'the place of becoming . . . of transformations, of the renewal of life'. In the Theban tombs the symbolic passage through this animal skin is frequently represented, and it is said that 'the deceased for whom this rite is performed will be reborn automatically'.

In the course of the Sed Festival the raising of the Djed column was replaced by the raising of obelisks. And in the Temple of Dendera where the Mysteries of Osiris are described, the erection of the Djed column took place on the final day of the ceremonies: at the same time as the Feast of Sokar, represented at

Medinet Habu across from the panegyrics of Min, in the course of which the King cuts a sheaf of spelt.

Whether it be a question of the Djed column or of obelisks, the oldest texts speak of the 'sacred rites, celebrated in conformity with this secret book of the art of the officiant' (called the Keeper of the Secret or Mystery), without providing any other explanation.

Left-hand page:

Illustrated on the ceiling of the Temple of Philae are several phases of the Osirian drama. After the lamentations of the weepers Isis and Nepthys (centre), the two sisters Selket and Douait reconstitute the body dismembered by Seth. They 'put the skeleton in order, purify the flesh, reunite the separated members', revive the corpse, and 'recall its soul'. The lion straddling the pylons framing the entry way reminds us that the rebirth of Osiris is linked to the Nile's flood which, Plutarch points out, took place when the sun was in Leo. The hawk-headed Sokar is laid out mummified on a platform held up by the Four Sons of Horus, protectors of the four organs of the human body, and

related also to the four cardinal points. (G. Bénédicte, *Le Temple de Philae*, pl. 40.)

Reliefs on the roof of the Temple of Dendera describe the applications of Nile water and of various unguents that must be made at each hour of the day and night in order to give Osiris back the use of his senses. Here also are enumerated the principal 'forms' under which Osiris was venerated in the sanctuaries in which his relics were kept. At Thebes, for example, lying on a bed decorated with lion's heads, the naked Osiris begins moving his legs and raises his hand to his forehead in a gesture of awakening, while at Coptos and at Dendera he is represented mummified with the white crown. (A. Mariette, *Dendera*, IV, pl. 68.)

At Abydos, jackal-headed Anubis, carrying a jar or unguent, prepares the mummy so as to render it incorruptible. At right, the mummified Osiris, stretched out between Isis and Horus, miraculously fecundates Isis, who hovers above him in the form of a kite. It is from this posthumous union, the legend says, that Horus, son of Isis, is born.

Right-hand page:

The Festival of Sokar. Sixteen priests in voluminous robes of pleated linen carry the *henu* barque of Sokar on their shoulders. Mentioned as early as the Pyramid Texts, this barque is considered 'archaic' because of its many oars, recalling those of the predynastic Gerzean-style boats (see p. 66). In front of the barque the King holds the centre of a cable to be pulled by sixteen figures in two rows, designated as follows: four familiars of the court, eight royal princes, four priests. This group recalls the erection of the Djed column, the King here seeming to take the role of the column. Two small priests turn toward him, waving incense as though he were himself the cult object. (*Medinet Habu*, University of Chicago Oriental Institute Publications, IV, pl. 196 b.)

This bas-relief in the Temple of Seti I at Abydos (c. 1300 BC) is the original representation of the fecundation of Isis in the form of a kite by the mummified Osiris from which the Dendera tableau (left) was taken. Horus – the future fruit of this posthumous union, but also an eternal principle – stands at his father Osiris' feet: 'Horus who protects Osiris, who fashions him by whom he himself was fashioned, who gives life to him by whom he himself was given life, who perpetuates the name of him by whom he himself was begotten'.

The birth of Horus thus symbolizes the promise of redemption offered to every human being. His different epithets evoke his triumph over the antinomies and the malefic powers, and express the possibility of liberation from the incessant cycles of death and rebirth. (A. Mariette, *Dendera*, IV, pl. 70.)

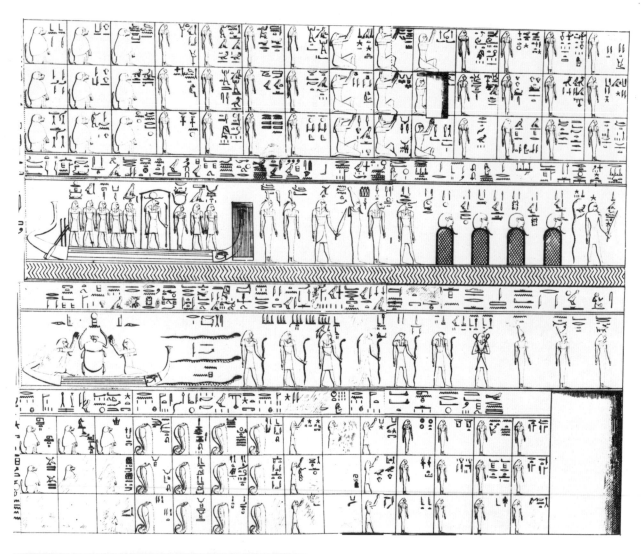

Death and metamorphosis

Writings of the Secret Chamber

'Writings of the secret chamber, the places where the souls, the divine entities, the shadows and the Spirits (the transfigured) stand. What they do. The beginning is the Horn of the West, the Gate of the Western Horizon. The end is utter darkness. . . .

'To know the souls of the Dwat, to know what they do, to know their transfigurations for Rê. To know the mysterious souls, to know what is in the Hours, their Neterw. To know what he calls out to them, to know the gates and roads by which the Great Neter passes. To know the course of the Hours and their entities. To know the sublime ones and the annihilated. . . .

'This is executed in the sacred place of the Dwat, following this form, being secret and hidden because of the small number of those who know it.'

The Book of What is in the Dwat opens with this summary of the Great Neter's progress, guided by the divine entities who are his own manifestations, through the 12 regions of the Dwat, which correspond to the 12 night hours. On the physical plane the Dwat is the region traversed by the

solar globe after having sunk below the western horizon. It is often written with a 'determinative' sign of an upside-down sky, thus evoking the southern hemisphere in which everything is actually inverted. On the abstract plane the Dwat corresponds conceptually to the place where Jesus rose from the dead, and it is in this sense that it is usually understood. On the psychic plane, however, the Dwat is 'the place of transformations', symbolized by the metamorphoses of the scarab. The scarab first exists as a worm or lava which can do nothing but absorb and digest food, then the cocoon is woven, within which, in complete stillness and without taking any food, the metamorphosis into a winged insect occurs.

The Great Neter descends into the Dwat in order, it is said, to 'gain knowledge of his own body'. He must go through all the phases of incarnation, from nutrition to metabolism, the transmutation of substance into vital energy and finally into subtle thought. The material support for this final stage is the spinal cord and cerebral matter, to which allusion is made in the final stage, the 12th hour of the night.

It is often repeated that the act of drawing these images by following the model will benefit the copyist both on earth and in the Dwat.

In the tombs of Thutmosis III and Amenophis II, the Book of What is in the Dwat is presented in the form of a huge papyrus unrolled on the walls around the burial chamber, here called 'the secret place of the Dwat'. In the tomb of Seti I, the 12 divisions are divided between the burial chamber and the various corridors, according to the nature of the hours described.

Shown here at left is the First Hour (Seti I), divided into four registers. On the upper register is a group of nine baboons who 'open to the Great Soul', then 12 female entities who sing the praises of 'Him who is in the earth'. Nine more worshipping figures follow, and finally 12 female guides, each bearing the name of one of the hours of the night. In the upper middle register is the solar barque in which we find, standing in the *naos* or tabernacle, the Great Neter in the form of a ram-headed figure, with a disc resting on his horns, who is given the name Flesh (Iwf). He is preceded in the barque by entities named respectively Opener of the Ways, Knowledge and Lady of the Barque, and followed by five entities among whom are

Hu (Word) and the pilot. Preceding the barque are two figures of Maât, a protector, Osiris, Sekhmet the Powerful, the Great Illuminer, then four chests symbolizing the four denominations of the phases of the daily cycle: Rê for noon, Atum for the evening, Khepri for dawn and Osiris for the night itself.

Below in the small skiff, the scarab Khepri between two figures of Osiris symbolizes the metamorphoses which are to take place in the darkness. This skiff is preceded by divinities related to vegetation. The lower register is occupied by a group of baboon musicians, by cobras who light the way by spitting fire, and by male and female worshippers.

On each side of the descending passageway in the tomb of Seti I are drawn 'the secret paths taken by the corpse of Sokar, invisible, mysterious image ... to which only Anubis [the embalmer] has access'. In the Fourth Hour these ways, called 'the corpse's expanse of water', are guarded by numerous serpents 'who crawl on their bellies' or who 'live from the breath of their mouths and the beating of their wings'. Iwf (Flesh) descends among them without seeing them, guided solely by the flames leaping from the mouths of the serpents at the prow and stern of his barque.

Left-hand page:

First Hour of the Book of What is in the Dwat, from the tomb of Seti, I c. 1300 BC. (M.G.Lefebure, *Le Tombeau de Seti Ier*, Mémoires publiées par les membres de la Mission archéologique française du Caire, 1882–1884, Paris 1886, IV, pl. 24, 25, 26.)

The pupa of the scarab, like the silkworm cocoon shown here, reveals the symbolism of Khepri: J.F. Fabre called it a 'striking image of the royal mummy wrapped in his strips of linen' (*Souvenirs entomologiques,* V, 84–85).

Right-hand page:

Fourth Hour of the Book of What is in the Dwat, from the tomb of Seti I, c. 1300 BC. (M.G.Lefebure, op. cit., Pl. 23, 24, 25.)

Death and metamorphosis

The Room of Gold

'House of Gold' or 'Room of Gold' was the name given to the workshops where statues, often decorated with metals and precious stones, were sculpted or 'given birth'. This epithet, however, was equally given to the burial chamber where another 'birth-giving' took place: the entry of the deceased into eternal life.

Certainly the discovery of the intact tomb of Tut-ankh-Amun offered archaeologists an unforgettable spectacle, but also it provided answers to many questions concerning the arrangement of the Room of Gold, since never before had one been found intact. For example, the plan of a royal tomb drawn on papyrus had indicated that the outer sarcophagus was enclosed in something, but scholars were far from imagining the reality. In fact, however, the pharaoh's mummy was found at the heart of *nine* successive envelopes.

Ornamented with many jewels and amulets, the mummy was resting in a first coffin covered in thick gold leaf. Swathed in a shroud and covered with necklaces and flower garlands, this was enclosed in two successive coffins decorated with gold and enamel, each

enveloped in a cloth, placed on a low, lion-headed bed. These three coffins rested in a quartzite sarcophagus whose four corners were protected by four tutelary female divinities, Isis, Nepthys, Neith and Selket. Then these four coffins were themselves enclosed in four shrines, the smaller nesting inside the larger, with the two largest separated by a linen veil strewn with gilt bronze daisies and placed on a baldachin, making a total of nine envelopes.

The burial chamber, oriented east-west, was preceded by an ante-chamber to the south, adjoining a storeroom. In front of the sealed wall giving access to the Room of Gold were found two statues of black varnished wood in the image of the king. The canes, sceptres, wigs, jewels and sandals of these statues were gilded.

Of the four shrines enclosing the sarcophagus, the outermost (whose roof recalls the double Sed Festival with its symbolism of rebirth) is entirely of gilt wood decorated with Djed columns (the symbol of Osiris) alternating with knots of Isis on a background of blue enamel. In the narrow corridor, separating the walls of the outermost shrine from the one inside it, were found the steering oars for celestial navigation.

The two emblems of Anubis occupying the west corners of the tomb (the side of the mummy's head) are the subject of many mysterious legends. They represent a skin enclosing the flesh which was said to be of gold and separated from the bones, said to be of silver. The divine cow Hesat (one of the forms of Isis) directed a stream of her milk at this skin, which is suspended from a stick planted in a bucket like a

pestle in its mortar. Making use of this instrument, Hesat made an unguent which gathered together and revivified the flesh of any dead person and caused him to be reborn, like Horus, as a young child (Jumilhac Papyrus XIII, 6).

Behind the linen drapery covering the third shrine, among the objects piled up against the door, an alabaster vase was found in the form of the *sma* symbol, representing the lungs at the end of the trachea. Two traditional Nile figures tie together the plant of the north, the kingdom of Horus (red crown), and the plant of the south, the territory of Seth (white crown). This symbol found in this place recalls that the 'transfiguration' of man is possible only after his victory over the antinomies through the union of opposites. The orientations of the vases are reversed with respect to the actual orientation of the tomb.

The outer shrine, like all the others, was closed by a bolt and sealed. Found on the inside of one of its double doors was the first chapter of the Book of the

Coming Forth into Day (Book of the Dead), concerning the ritual of placing the dead in the tomb, and on the other door, Chapter 134 of this same book, intended to repulse any enemy or partisan of Seth, and to enable the deceased to sail in the company of Rê.

The exterior and interior walls and ceilings of the shrines are covered with a seemingly random selection of extracts from the principal 'sacred books', along with several representations found nowhere else, all placed in no apparent sequence. A closer examination of their distribution, however, reveals an artful grouping of carefully chosen 'themes' on either side of the narrow aisle between the successive shrines, nested one within the other, so that the inscriptions on one wall are found to be completed by those of the wall facing it.

The ancient priests numbered the shrines by beginning with the smallest, and in like manner the principal themes can be enumerated, going from the interior toward the exterior:

1: Evocation of Cosmogenesis, starting from the primordial Ocean.
2: The process of Incarnation, expressed by the presence of the Four Sons of Horus, protectors of the principal organs indispensable for physical life.
3: The process of becoming conscious, suggested by the triumph over obstacles and by the mention of Maât, once with respect to the Origin, and once with respect to the Return.
4: The Return to the cosmic source with the enrichment of lived experience.

The representations of the birth of the solar globe which cover the outer walls of the third shrine are of exceptional interest, for they are found nowhere else. Accompanied by intentionally enigmatic inscriptions, they appear to be an attempt to account for cosmic phenomena in 'physical' terms.

Left-hand page:

The tomb of King Tut-ankh-Amun in the course of opening, 1923. (Howard Carter, *The Tomb of Tut-ankh-Amun*, London 1923–30, II, pl. x.)

Oars and other sacred objects between the outer shrines. (Howard Carter, op. cit., pl. 5.)

Emblem or *nebris* of Anubis. (Howard Carter, op. cit., II, pl. 6.)

Archaeologists open the outermost shrine. (Howard Carter, op. cit., II, pl. 13.)

Right-hand page:

Unguent vase inside outermost shrine. (Howard Carter, op. cit., II, pl. x.)

The third shrine (second to be opened). (Cairo Museum.)

The enigmatic tableau on the third shrine. (A. Piankoff, *Les Chapelles de Tut-ankh-Amun*, Paris 1952, pl. 4.)

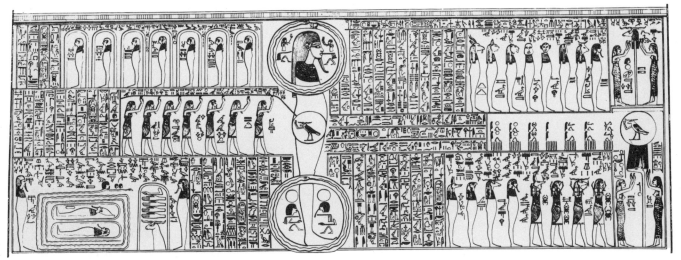

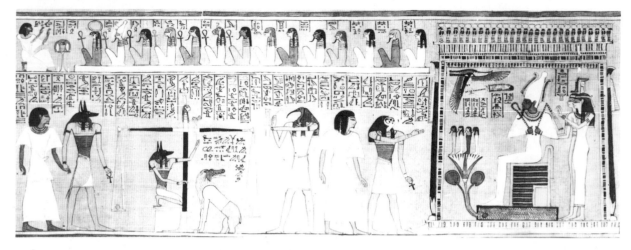

Death and metamorphosis

The Book of the Coming Forth into Day

In the Book of the Coming Forth into Day, after the procession to the necropolis, the funeral and the hymns, there follow incantations intended to set aside all obstacles to the dead person's ascension to the sky. Then formulae are recited to 'open the tomb', so that the dead person, identified with Osiris-Orion, may 'walk on earth among the living', and neither he nor his name will ever perish. All the celestial powers are invoked so that the soul, *ba*, may return to see the mummy in the Kingdom of the Dead and unite with its *ka* (or double); and that it be not kept prisoner by the guardians of the shadows of the dead nor expelled from the sky.

In the famous Judgment Scene, called the Psychostasia, the deceased is brought forward, either by Maât or by Anubis. The scale is surmounted by Maât, Justice; on one of its pans is the heart of the deceased, and Maât's feather on the other. The human passions must not weigh too heavily, nor must the appetites (expressed by the *ka*) reattract too strongly, or it may be that the female monster, the 'Devourer', would gobble up the deceased, who anxiously awaits the judgment to be rendered by Thoth (with ibis-head) in the presence of Osiris. It is in this 'Hall of the Double Maât' (individual consciousness and cosmic consciousness) that the famous Negative Confession takes place, in the course of which the Osiris-Name (the deceased) declares himself to have been charitable on earth under all circumstances, and exonerates himself, in the presence of 42 judges, from having committed any of 42 faults. Horus then introduces him to Osiris, seated on a throne resting on a pool of water, out from which grows a lotus-flower supporting the Four Sons of Horus, protectors of the four principal organs of the body.

Left-hand page:

Scene of the 'Psychostasia' illustrating Chapter 125 of the Book of the Coming Forth into Day. (Hunefer Papyrus, British Museum, London.)

Statue of the royal *Ka* of King Horus Dachur (Twelfth Dynasty, 2000 BC). (Cairo Museum.)

Image of the royal mummy of Tut-ankh-Amun, lying on the ritual lion-headed bed. The falcon Horus perches on one side of him, and the *ba*-bird with human head on the other. (Cairo Museum.)

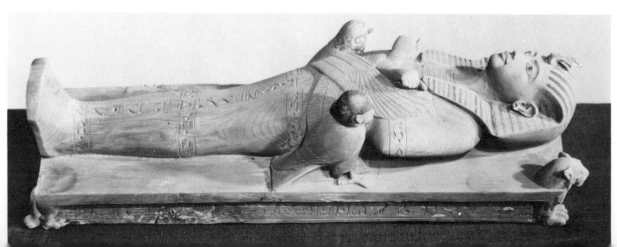

The treasury

The small eastern chamber in Tut-ankh-Amun's tomb communicating with the Room of Gold was called the 'Treasury' by the excavators because it contained the most precious objects. It had no door but instead seemed to be guarded by the splendid dog jackal Anubis in black wood with details in gold, alabaster, obsidian and silver, lying on a gilt wooden coffer containing ritual objects.

Anubis, 'he who is on the mysteries', is the guardian of the sacred and secret writings. Under the names of 'chief of the divine pavilion' and 'he who is in the strip of cloth', he presides over embalmment. Under the name of 'Opener of the Ways' he steers the solar boat as it makes its daily reappearance.

Behind him is the large gilt wooden head of the sacred celestial cow with its copper lyriform horns painted black. Symbol of the heavens, Hathor or Mehet-wrt, who welcomes the deceased to her breast, is outlined against the famous canopic chest.

Under a dais topped with *uraei*, a chest in gilt wood, itself surmounted by a cornice of raised cobras, covers the splendid alabaster chest containing the four miniature coffins in gold with enamel work which contained the dead king's four essential internal organs.

Right-hand page:

General view of the Treasury. Howard Carter, *The Tomb of Tut-ankh-Amun*, III, pl. 2.

The Four Sons of Horus

The four birds which are released at the coronation of the Horus-King bear the names and distinctive heads of the Four Sons of Horus, protectors of the four principal organs of the body. They are themselves guarded by four female protective divinities. Each flies towards one of the cardinal points, which are given in the following order:

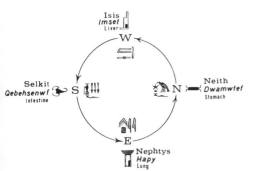

'Imset: go to the south and announce to the divinities of the south that the Horus [the king] has taken the White Crown and has united it with the Red Crown.

'Hâpi: go to the North and say to the divinities of the North . . .

'Dwa-mwt-f: go to the West and say to the divinities of the West . . .

'Kebehsenwf: go to the East and say to the divinities of the East . . .'

Imset, with human head, is protector of the liver and is under the guardianship of Isis, and Isis is said to come from the west (Pyramid Texts, 1255).

Hâpi, with baboon's head, is protector of the lungs, and is under the guardianship of Nepthys who, according to the same source, comes from the east.

Dwa-mwt-f, with dog or jackal head, is protector of the stomach, and is under the guardianship of Neith, divinity of weaving and of the red crown of the north.

Kebehsenwf, with falcon's head, is protector of the intestines, and is thus under the guardianship of Selket, the scorpion divinity, called 'she who causes the throat to breathe', and who is associated with the white crown of the south (Pyramid Texts, 1375).

This arrangement, suggested by the texts, is actually that of the female divinities encircling the outer Canopic Chest of gilded wood in Tut-ankh-Amun's tomb. The 'function' of each of these divinities then reveals itself as follows:

Imset, with human head, protector of the liver, under the guardianship of *Isis* at the west, is the steward par excellence. From the material received by the stomach (which precedes the liver) he stores what is necessary for the manufacture of sugar, fats, the albumens and urea. He thriftily sets aside the iron from the used red corpuscles to be reutilized at a given time, and he transforms their haemoglobin into bilirubin, the pigment

Continued overleaf

which colours the bile which he secretes in large quantity. Finally, 'he goes to the south' to bring to Kebehsenwf, the guardian of the intestines, the bile which is indispensible for digestion and excretion, an important antitoxin.

Kebehsenwf, with the falcon head, presides then over the production of the white chyle in the intestine, under the guardianship of the scorpion Selket of the south. Much could be said of this insect, which devours her mate after the nuptial consummation, but which, because of her maternal vigilance, is sometimes assimilated to Isis. Her children are born in a thin membrane, and when their mother liberates them they cling on to her back where they develop by *tripling* in volume *without taking in any food,* other than by osmosis. A great part of the white chyle produced in the small intestine also circulates by osmosis; furthermore, the intestine's function of separating the assimilable elements from the waste products requires a great sensitivity involving the development of an entire defensive reflex system (sympathetic and cerebro-spinal). The scorpion's venom attacks precisely the nervous system, a remarkable instance of symbolic analogy. Kebehsenwf sends the white chyle from the south to the east, to the left subclavian vein.

Hâpi, with Nepthys of the east, protects the lungs. It would be difficult to understand why he is given the head of the baboon, sacred to Thoth, master of time, if his name did not give us the clue. *Hap* means 'to circulate'. Since the heart was always left in place in the mummy, the lungs were taken to symbolize the entire system of red blood circulation whose rhythm (pulsation and breath) was regulated by Hâpi. He receives the *white* lymphatic fluid transported by the vessels gathered in the thoracic canal then deposited in the left sub-clavian vein where it is mixed with the *red* blood and participates with it in the gas exchange and oxygenation which takes place in the lungs. The union of the red and the white is symbolized by the hieroglyphic sign *sma*, representing the lungs suspended at the end of the trachea, around which are knotted the plants of the north and the south, emphasizing the vegetal character of the respiratory function (see p. 90).

Dwa-mwt-f, with the head of a dog or jackal, protects the stomach under the guardianship of Neith, divinity of the north and of weaving. The dog has the role of transforming what was originally foreign matter into living substance under the influence of particular secretions. The dog is famous for its sense of smell which recalls the role played by odour in stimulating the secretion of the juices necessary for digestion. Also, the jackal has the particularity of *eating meat in a state of decomposition,* and it is he who, by virtue of analogies, is the sovereign master of mummification, the principal goal of which is to prevent decomposition.

The quartzite sarcophagus has these same divinities grouped differently, this time by pairs: Isis and Nepthys at the head, Neith and Selket at the feet. In this arrangement the opposing orientations and the complementary functions are paired:
– At the north, the stomach receives from the exterior and digests under the guardianship of Neith.
– At the south, the intestine digests and rejects to the exterior under the guardianship of Selket.
– At the east in the lungs the haemoglobin (red) is aerobic, with Nepthys.
– At the west, in the liver, the bilirubin (green) is anaerobic, with Isis.

Left-hand page:

Scorpion with head of Isis. Bronze sceptre head. (Baltimore Museum.)

Alabaster canopic chest of Tut-ankh-Amun, shown without its lid. (Howard Carter, *The Tomb of Tut-ankh-Amun,* London 1923–30, III, pl. 10. Cairo Museum.)

'This graceful figure portrays the goddess Selket whose emblem, a scorpion, is placed on her head.' (*Treasures of Tutankhamun,* New York exhibition catalogue, pl. 24.)

Canopic coffin of Tut-ankh-Amun. Each of the four vital organs was mummified, wrapped in strips of cloth and placed in a gold-and-enamel miniature coffin within a cylindrical recess in the canopic chest. This was closed with a human-headed stopper like those shown at left; later, after the Eighteenth Dynasty, three out of each set of four stoppers were given jackal heads. (Howard Carter, op. cit., III, pl. 11. Cairo Museum.)

Death and resurrection

I THE CANOPIC CHEST

The position of the female protective divinities around the outer gilded wooden chest corresponds to their theoretic orientation and to their actual placement in the tomb. Isis at the west, Selket at the south, Nepthys at the east and Neith at the north in conformity with the planar vision of the cross of the orientations.

But the 'House of Life' described by Salt Papyrus 825 adds a third vertical axis which suggests envisioning the chest spatially: 'A figure standing in a cube. His two arms are extended following the east-west (Nepthys-Isis) axis and his feet are in stride in the perpendicular direction north-south (Neith-Selket).' This arrangement corresponds to that of the divinities paired at the corners of the inner alabaster chest where the orientations are reversed.

The figure in the cube is thus striding to the south, on the path of the cyclic return of death and regeneration represented by Osiris-Orion.

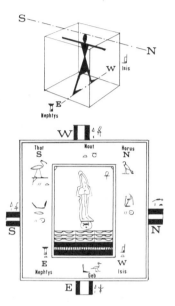

III THE ROOM OF GOLD

The Burial Chamber of Tut-ankh-Amun is oriented in such a way that the head is at the east. The female divinities protecting the quartzite sarcophagus are grouped in pairs: Isis and Nepthys at the corners near the shoulders and Selket and Neith at the corners near the feet and correctly aligned on the true N-S axis in such a way that the figure drawn in the cube is striding towards the north. Now the opposing directions indicated by the sarcophagus (containing the mummy) and the canopic chest (the organs) recall the two ways marked by the two air shafts in the King's Chamber of the pyramid of Cheops, and the royal tombs of the First Dynasty, where the symbolism was pushed to the point of building two tombs: one in the south for the viscera, and the other in the north for the mummy – in relation with the 'imperishable' circumpolar stars of the northern sky, and thus with liberation and immortality.

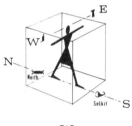

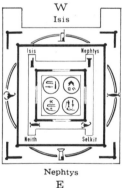

II THE HOUSE OF LIFE

'The House of Life. It is at Abydos composed of four bodies . . . [which are] Isis on one side, Nepthys on the other, Horus at the third and Thoth at the last. These are the four corners. Geb is the ground, Nut the Sky. The Great Hidden God rests in the interior' (Salt Papyrus 825 VI, 6–9). The papyrus then describes the four doors opening on to the four cardinal points and the general orientation of the edifice corresponds to that of the 'Room of Gold' in Tut-ankh-Amun's tomb.

The comparison between the two documents shows the following divergences: here Isis and Nepthys occupy the corners at the side of the feet, and Horus and Thoth (who here takes Seth's place) as Lords of the North and South occupy the corners near the head. The small figure in the cube then will indicate the N-S axis with his arms, and will be striding from east to west, following the course of the stars and the apparent revolution of the sun.

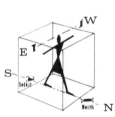

Further reading

Alliot, M. *Le Culte d'Horus à Edfou au temps des Ptolémées (Institut français d'Archéologie orientale)*. Cairo 1954.

Assmann, J. *Zeit und Ewigkeit im alten Ägypten*. Heidelberg 1975.

Badawy, A. *Le Dessin architectural chez les anciens Egyptiens*. Cairo 1968. *A History of Egyptian Architecture*. Berkeley and Los Angeles 1954–1968.

Barguet, P. *Le Livre des Morts des anciens Egyptiens*. Paris 1967.

Bleeker, C.J. *Historia Religionum. Handbook for the History of Religions*. Leiden 1969–1971.

Bonneau, D. *La Crue du Nil, divinité égyptienne, à travers mille ans d'histoire*. Paris 1964.

Breasted, J.H. *Ancient Records of Egypt*. Chicago 1906, 1962. *Development of Religion and Thought in Ancient Egypt*. New York 1912, 1972.

Budge, E.A.W. *The Gods of the Egyptians*. London 1904. *Osiris. The Egyptian Religion of Resurrection*. New Hyde Park 1961.

Carter, H. *The Tomb of Tut-Ankh-Amen*. Norwich 1923–1930.

Clark, R.T.R. *Myth and Symbol in Ancient Egypt*. London 1978.

Daumas, F. *La Civilisation de l'Egypte pharaonique*. Paris 1967.

Derchain, P. *Le Papyrus Salt 825. Rituel pour la conservation de la vie en Egypte*. Brussels 1965. *Mythes et dieux lunaires. Sources orientales*. Brussels 1962.

Desroches-Noblecourt, C. *Vie et mort d'un pharaon*. Paris 1967.

Drioton, E., and J. Vandier. *L'Egypte* (5th edn), Paris 1975.

Dunand, F. *Les Mystères égyptiens*, in *Mystères et syncretismes. Etudes d'histoire des religions*. Paris 1975.

Edwards, I.E.S. *The Pyramids of Egypt*. Harmondsworth 1947, 1964.

Elisofon, E. *Le Nil*. Paris-Lausanne. 1964.

Faulkner, R.O. *The Ancient Egyptian Coffin Texts*. Warminster 1978. *The Papyrus Bremner-Rhind (B.M. 10188)*. Brussels 1933.

Festugière, R.P. *La Révélation d'Hermès Trismégiste*. Paris 1949.

Gardiner, A.H. *Egypt of the Pharaohs*. Oxford 1972.

Griffiths, J.G. *Plutarch's De Iside et Osiride, with an introduction, translation and commentary*. Cardiff 1970. *The Conflict of Horus and Seth*. Liverpool 1960.

Guilmot, M. *Le Message spirituel de l'Egypte ancienne*. Paris 1970. *Les initiés et les rites initiatiques en Egypte ancienne*. Paris 1977.

Hickmann, H. *Musicologie pharaonique. Etudes sur l'évolution de l'art musical dans l'Egypte ancienne*. Kehl 1956. *Instruments de musique*. Cairo 1949. *45 siècles de musique dans l'Egypte ancienne*. Paris 1956.

Hornung, E. *Das Amduat*. Wiesbaden 1963. *Die Eine und die Vielen*. Darmstadt 1973.

Iversen, E. *Canon and Proportions in Egyptian art*. Warminster 1975.

Jequier, G. *Manuel d'archéologie égyptienne: Architecture*. Paris 1924.

Landstrom, B. *Ships of the Pharaohs*. London 1970.

Lauer, J.P. *Saqqarah*. Paris, London 1976.

Lefebvre, G. *Romans et contes égyptiens de l'époque pharaonique*. Paris 1949, 1976.

Legrain, G. *Louqsor sous les Pharaons (Légendes)*. Paris and Brussels 1914.

Mariette, A.E. *Denderah. Description du grand temple*. Paris 1870–1880.

Maspéro, G. *The Dawn of Civilization*. Transl. M.L. McClure. London 1894, 1968.

Massoulard, E. *Préhistoire et protohistoire d'Egypte*. Paris 1949.

Mekhitarian, A. *L'Egypte (Religions du Monde)*. Paris 1964.

Michalowski, K. *Art of Ancient Egypt*. London, New York 1969.

Montet, P. *Eternal Egypt*. New York 1969.

Morenz, S. *La Religion égyptienne*. Paris 1977.

Mercer, S.A.B. *Horus. Royal God of Egypt*. Grafton, Mass. 1942.

Moret, A. *Du caractère religieux de la Royauté pharaonique*. Paris 1902. *Rois et dieux d'Egypte*. Paris 1916. *Mystères égyptiens*. Paris 1913.

Müller, W.M. *Egyptian Mythology*. New York 1964.

Murray, M.A. *Splendour that was Egypt*. London 1972.

Pace, M.M. *Wrapped for Eternity. The Story of the Egyptian Mummy*. New York 1974.

Parker, R.A. *The Calendars of Ancient Egypt*. Chicago 1950. *Egyptian Astronomical Texts*. London 1960.

Piankoff, A. *The Tomb of Ramsses VI (Bollingen Series)*. New York 1954. *La Création du disque solaire*. Cairo 1953. *The Shrines of Tut-Ankh-Amun*. New York 1955. *The Litany of Re*. New York 1964.

Pirenne, J. *Histoire de la civilisation de l'Egypte ancienne*. Neuchâtel, Paris 1961.

Posener, G. *Dictionnaire de la civilisation égyptienne*. Paris 1959.

Sauneron, S. *Les Prêtres de l'ancienne Egypte*. Paris 1957. *Les Fêtes religieuses d'Esna aux derniers siècles du paganisme*. Cairo 1962.

Schwaller de Lubicz, R.A. *Le Temple de l'Homme Apet du Sud à Louqsor*. Paris 1977. *Le Roi de la Théocratie pharaonique*. Paris 1958. *Symbole et symbolique*. Paris, New York, 1978.

Schwaller de Lubicz, I. *Her-Bak. Egyptian Initiate*. London, New York, 1978.

Sethe, K. *Übersetzung und Kommentar zu den altägyptischen Pyramidentexten*. Hamburg 1962.

Te Velde, H. *Seth, God of Confusion*. Leiden 1967.

Vandier, J. *La Religion égyptienne*. Paris 1944. *Manuel d'Archéologie égyptienne*. (6 Vol.) Paris 1955–78.

Yoyotte, J. *La Naissance du Monde selon l'Egypte ancienne*. Paris 1959.

Acknowledgments

The objects in the plates, pp. 33–64, are in the collections of Brussels, Musées Royaux du Cinquantenaire 55 below; Cairo Museum 43 below, 44, 45; London, British Museum 42, 46, Paris, Louvre 39.

Photographs were supplied by Michel Andrain 80 below; Archives Photographiques, Paris 67 r.; Chicago University, Oriental Institute 40–41, 72 below, 73 below; Bruce Colman 72 above l,; Dayton 33; Documentation Photographique, Paris 39 r., 67 above and below l.; Andrzej Dziewanowski 72 above r.; Egypt Exploration Society, London 38, 38–39, 48–49, 50–51, 51, 68 below, 69 below, 83 above; Werner Forman 55 below, 84 above l.; Gaddis 47; Griffith Institute, Ashmolean Museum, Oxford 43 below, 90 (4 ills), 91 above l. and r., 93 above, 94 above r. and below l., centre and r.; Robert Harding 44, 45, 62–63 below, 92 below; André Held 55 above; Hirmer 34–35 above, 43 above, 52, 53, 54, 71 above l., 76 above, 77 above, 82 l., 83 centre, 84 below, 87 below, 92 centre; Kersting 36–37, 37, below; William MacQuitty 34–35 below, 56–57 above, 58, 60–61, 62–63 below, 64, 80 above l., Metropolitan Museum of Art, New York 59; Albert Shoucair 37 above r.; Jean Vertut 57 r.; Roger Viollet 83 below.